HACKER'S EDGE

Breaking Rules, Beating Odds, and Reinventing a Life

Ryan Merket

COMAL
PUBLISHING

Author's Note

This book is a memoir. It is a work of nonfiction based on my memory of the events and people described. I have done my best to recreate conversations and scenes as they happened, but I acknowledge that memory is a subjective and often imperfect lens. The story is a reflection of my personal experiences and my truth.

In some cases, names and identifying characteristics of individuals have been changed to protect their privacy. Any resemblance to persons with these new names is purely coincidental.

ISBN-13: 979-8-9931013-0-9

Cover design by: Ryan Merket

Printed in the United States of America

To my parents: Thank you for never stop believing in me.

Jenn: thanks for coming on this crazy ride with me.

Matt Pendergraff: you were the first to give this little-big PHP dev a shot. Thank you. "Lucky!"

Kris Wainscott / Norbert Hendrikse: thanks for showing me a new way and being there for me through countless startups.

Erik Moore: you wrote the first check and have been by my side through every startup. Huge thank you.

Nalin Mittal: more than a cofounder you are a real friend, confidant, mentor, and advisor all in one. Thank you.

Nick Laning: more than a brother, I owe a lot of this to you pushing me to be a better person.

Heath Black: your words have got me out of some really dark places. Thank you for always being there.

Micah Baldwin: proud to call you a mentor, friend, and confidant. Thank you.

David Cochran: professors like you are the reason universities should exist. Thank you.

CONTENTS

FOREWORD

When I first met Ryan Merket through Techstars, he was working at Amazon, and something about him immediately stood out. In a world filled with pretenders and wannabe entrepreneurs, Ryan was different—he was the real deal. He had built, operated, and successfully exited a company. More importantly, he carried himself with the quiet confidence that only comes from having been in the trenches and emerged victorious.

What struck me most about Ryan wasn't just his impressive track record, but his genuine desire to share what he'd learned. Over the years, he became both an investor in my company and an invaluable mentor. When it came time to pursue the sale of my own venture, Ryan was there, guiding me through complexities I never would have navigated alone. He taught me lessons that business schools don't cover and insights that only come from real-world experience.

Our earliest conversations often drifted to hacking

and technology—topics that revealed Ryan's deep understanding of systems, both digital and human. He wasn't just talking theory; he had lived it. He understood the hacker mentality not as destruction, but as a way of seeing opportunities where others see obstacles, of finding unconventional paths to solutions.

In *Hacker's Edge*, Ryan shares the raw, unfiltered story of how he forged his own path through entrepreneurship and life. This isn't another sanitized business book filled with generic advice. It's an honest account of what it really takes to break rules, beat odds, and reinvent yourself in an industry that's constantly evolving.

The tech world is unfortunately filled with noise—people who talk a good game but have never built anything meaningful. Ryan cuts through all of that. He's been there, done it, and earned the right to share these insights. In these pages, you'll find the kind of hard-won wisdom that can only come from someone who has faced real challenges, made tough decisions, and emerged stronger.

Whether you're an aspiring entrepreneur, a seasoned business owner, or someone simply looking to understand what it takes to succeed in our digital age, Ryan's story will challenge your assumptions and inspire you to think differently about what's possible.

I'm forever grateful for Ryan's mentorship and friendship. His guidance helped me achieve my own exit, and I know the lessons in this book will do the same for countless others ready to find their own hacker's edge.

Marcus J. Carey
Cybersecurity Entrepreneur

INTRODUCTION

Serendipity at a Sushi Bar in
Bangalore

The universe has a twisted sense of humor. There I was, 33 years old, grabbing drinks at Shiro's sushi restaurant in Bangalore, India—a place rumored to have good cocktails halfway across the world. I was with a coworker I'd known casually back in San Francisco. As we were chopping it up, the conversation drifted to where we grew up.

"I grew up in Sacramento," he said.

"No way," I shot back, "When I was a kid, I lived in Sacramento!"

He nodded. "Yeah, but it was a little suburb called Rancho Cordova…"

My jaw tightened. "I lived in Rancho Cordova!"

"Oh wow," he said, a bit surprised. "But yeah, I went to a really small Catholic school there."

This was getting weird. "I went to Catholic school in Rancho Cordova!"

"Huh, wild. St. Joh…"

"…John Vianney?" I finished, "I went to St. John Vianney in Rancho Cordova!"

We both just stared at each other, the noise of the Bangalore bar fading.

"Wait," I said, "how old are you?"

"Thirty-two…"

"I'm thirty-two… Wait a minute." The gears were grinding, disbelief warring with a dawning, insane possibility. "Were we in the same class?! Do you know Matt Whalen?"

His eyes widened. "No way…"

Speechless. We just stood there in disbelief. I fumbled for my phone, remembering a couple of old friends on Facebook from those two years at St. John Vianney. I hammered out a quick post about the insane coincidence. Sure enough, within minutes, others chimed in, confirming that he and I were, in fact, in the same class for two whole years. We'd even played on the same goddamn basketball team. Someone even dug up an old yearbook, snapping a photo of us on the same page, two decades prior.

And there we were, more than twenty years later, sitting at a sushi bar in Bangalore, India. It was wild. Unbelievable.

Life had taken me from rock bottom to globetrotting techie, and in that bizarre moment, it felt like fate was winking at me, reminding me how impossibly random and beautifully fucked up my journey had been.

HACKER'S
EDGE

BREAKING RULES, BEATING ODDS, AND REINVENTING A LIFE

Ryan Merket

PART I: FORGING THE EDGE

CHAPTER 1:
THE SAFETY OF
THE MACHINE

My obsession with understanding systems started before I could properly read. In first grade, my dad's Commodore 64 was my playground, and the games that came on floppy disks were my puzzles. I figured out how to load classics like *Might and Magic*, but I'd always hit a wall: a prompt on the screen demanding a specific word from the thick, printed manual. It was a simple form of copy protection, designed to stop kids from just passing around copied disks. For me, it was the first lock I ever needed to pick.

I couldn't decode the full sentences, but I could see patterns. I'd sit on the floor, flipping through the manual, matching the shapes of the words on the screen to the text on the page until I found the one that fit. When the word worked and the game finally roared to life, the feeling was electric. It wasn't hacking, not yet. But it was the first taste of a powerful idea:

Every system has rules, and if you're patient and clever enough, you can figure them out. It was the beginning of a lifelong obsession with finding the hidden keys to unlock any world I wanted to enter. I was hooked.

The real world, however, had its own set of rules, and they were far more brutal and unpredictable. I remember one afternoon walking home from school in Rancho Cordova, reaching the crosswalk on Coloma Road I used every day, and then chaos erupted. A red car, moving way too fast, smashed violently into the back of a metro bus. The sound was sickening. The guy in the car wasn't wearing a seatbelt. I saw blood, so much blood, splattered across his dash and the blown-out windshield. I just stood there, frozen, staring for what felt like an eternity before a parent rushed over, grabbed me, and whisked me back to school grounds. The image was seared into my brain.

That same busy road would become a source of even more personal trauma. I had just gotten home from school one day when the phone rang. It was our neighbors. Their voices were panicked. They said my older brother, Matt, had been in a really bad accident and they were taking him to the hospital. They told me to wait outside; they were coming to get me because my parents were heading there directly from work. I was in shock. I had no idea what happened. I just stood there, frozen.

When the neighbors' large, light-blue van pulled up, they opened the door and told me to get inside. As we sped away, they told me what they had seen. Matt was in a crosswalk on Coloma Road when a Jeep got a green light and gunned it, running him over and dragging him for nearly 30 feet before stopping. My brother was conscious but his femur was a compound fracture, the bone piercing through his skin. He was scraped up everywhere.

The next few weeks were a blur of antiseptic smells and hushed conversations in the hospital. My brother went through a radical new procedure where a surgeon inserted a metal rod into his femur, allowing the bone to grow back around it. In a moment of unbelievable serendipity, it turned out the surgeon who pioneered this technique happened to go to our church. He took my brother's case and provided exceptional care. But the damage was done. My brother, an incredible athlete, never played sports again. The event was emotionally traumatizing for him and for our entire family. It was really, really hard.

The world's veneer of safety kept ripping open. Around that same time, I was in 5th grade when I chased the ice cream truck down the street after a baseball game. As I stood in line, two men got out of a car, pulled what my 10-year-old brain registered as an Uzi, and robbed the driver. I ran. I pedaled my bike harder than I ever had, my heart hammering against my ribs, convinced they were going to kill me. I burst into the house, screaming and sobbing. The police later asked me, a 10-year-old kid, to return to the scene to be a witness. For weeks, I was terrified they'd come back for me, peeking through the blinds at night, convinced I was being watched.

All of these traumatic episodes—the sudden violence I witnessed, the accident that shattered my brother's body, the helplessness of being robbed at gunpoint—pushed me towards computers and the safety of the digital world. It was a place where I could control the inputs and outputs, be anyone I wanted to be, and do anything I wanted to do. The real world was dangerously unpredictable; online, I could escape to a land I controlled.

But I wasn't just a basement hacker. I also had a deep love for sports. I played soccer, baseball, tackle football—I lived for the scoreboard. If there was a way to win, I'd find it. My life became a study in contrasts. After my family moved to New Braunfels, my summers were spent in the idyllic chaos of the Guadalupe River, a floating party of Jell-O shots, beer bongs, and classic rock. We would build rope swings and tag along with college kids, hacking the social systems of the river to earn our keep in free booze. Those were the best summers of my life, a different kind of escape.

But those earlier memories—the wreck, my brother's broken body, the robbery—never left me. They taught me how quickly things can turn, how thin the line is between safety and chaos. And maybe that's why I always worked so hard to control systems—to build things, to plan, to lead.

Because deep down, I know what it's like when things fall apart. And I've been building ever since.

CHAPTER 2: MY BUSINESS SCHOOL WAS IRC

Long before I worked at Facebook, before one of the early employees at Reddit, before Amazon, before I'd ever heard the term "Series A" or "burn rate," my first startup wasn't built in a dusty Silicon Valley garage. It was forged in the flickering glow of IRC chatrooms, across a global network of FTP servers, and immortalized in the intricate ASCII art of .NFO files. I wasn't pitching VCs with a polished deck; I was cold messaging seasoned crackers across multiple time zones, trying to recruit them to build a crew based on skill, reputation, and a shared obsession.

It all started in high school, those years when I progressively stopped attending actual classes because geometry and history just couldn't hold a candle to the siren song of learning Assembly.

I spent my days (and most nights) reverse-engineering software, teaching myself the arcane arts of debuggers, binary patching, and encryption. Eventually, my growing skills earned me an invitation to join an established cracking group —a private, invite-only crew dedicated to dissecting and removing copy protections from commercial software. It was a thrilling, clandestine world. And within a year, I did what every future founder instinctively does eventually: I left and decided to start my own.

Building a top-tier cracking group from scratch required every ounce of the hustle, strategy, and operational rigor that any legitimate startup demands. First, we had to choose a name— something original, sharp, and instantly respected by others in "the scene." This wasn't trivial; names carried weight, names like ORiON, CLASS, or PREMiUM. Ours had to be just as good, if not better. It had to signal credibility and skill from the moment someone saw it.

Next came branding. We collaborated with talented ASCII artists from the DEMO scene to create our group's unique logo and visual identity, rendered in the iconic .NFO format—that 8-bit art file that accompanied every single release, burned forever into the underground digital archive. The file_id.diz was our digital shipping label, the critical metadata that every top-tier FTP server needed to index and distribute our work across the globe.

Recruiting was real work, a constant challenge. You couldn't just hang out at a coffee shop and find a C++ developer with a penchant for reverse engineering. You had to master the nuances of IRC communication, know how to approach and vet potential members, prove your own worth, and build deep trust with complete strangers scattered across continents—all for absolutely zero pay. No equity, no stock options, no upside beyond the sheer passion for the craft and the prestige of being part of an elite crew.

Once we had our squad, we ran operations like a well-oiled, albeit illicit, business. We held weekly meetings in private IRC channels or chatrooms. We used bots, often custom-written in TCL, to track "supply" (newly released, uncracked software), assign cracking tasks to members based on their skills, push completed releases out to our distribution network, and even manage rudimentary version control. We built automations to package our cracked files correctly and populate the metadata in our .NFOs with meticulous precision. We had partnerships —informal, often unspoken alliances with other specialized groups. They might crack a particularly tough RSA key for us; we'd return the favor by sourcing a rare piece of software they needed. This was all in the 1990s mind you, way before the time of AI.

And just like any startup, we had our share of "HR" issues: key members ghosting mid-release, internal political drama, accusations of poaching talent between rival groups. It was chaotic. It was demanding. It was glorious. And we scaled— fast. At our peak, my group was responsible for releasing around 150 distinct cracked software packages a month.

Patches to .exe files or our own stand alone apps that code generate valid serial numbers for software, called keygens, we did whatever it took to turn software to free. Keygens always took priority as it was considered a cleaner crack in not having to change the target .exe file to circumvent the copy protection.

People talk about MBAs. My business school was a cracked copy of mIRC (the IRC chat client) and a global

team of hackers I'd never met. We didn't do it for money. We did it for the game.

In that underground world, you had to motivate your members. We created leaderboards, accessible with a simple !leaderboard command in our IRC channel, tracking who was the top supplier, the most prolific cracker, the fastest releaser —all core roles. The banter and competition were fierce and constant. If your group put out a major release, you celebrated, even if it was just virtual high-fives across time zones.

Beyond internal competition, we were in a relentless race with other groups. If you were second to release a title, your release was "nuked"—summarily deleted from all the top FTP sites. No points for second place. There were even websites dedicated to tracking which groups put out the most releases, and of what type.

We all woke up dreaming of being at the top of those charts. That raw, competitive drive, that desire for recognition within our subculture, was an incredibly powerful motivator, something traditional environments often forget when they assume compensation is the only lever.

Looking back, that was my real business school. I learned how to form and lead teams, build complex operational systems, automate relentlessly, and negotiate high-stakes partnerships— all before I even had a driver's license.

Eventually, though, I had a moment of profound clarity, a turning point.

I realized that the work I was doing, for all its technical brilliance and intellectual stimulation, was fundamentally hurting people—software developers, creators, artists, people just like me trying to earn a living and feed their families from their craft.

That realization hit hard. I pivoted. I walked away from the scene and, as you know, eventually enrolled in college. In my spare time then, I started using my skills for the other side: helping those same developers secure their code, advising on stronger copy protections and better encryption techniques to try and stop the next generation of teenage pirates.

But that underground startup, that "business school of IRC," gave me an operating rhythm, a way of thinking about systems and efficiency, that I've never let go of. At every legitimate company I've joined since, I've instinctively looked for ways to build tools, streamline internal operations, and improve communication.

Because if a bunch of teenagers scattered across the globe, armed with nothing but their wits, a dial-up modem (initially), and a cracked copy of mIRC, could organize a complex global software supply chain with custom bots and a relentless focus on execution, what possible excuse does your average Series A startup have for being sloppy or inefficient?

People talk a lot about traditional business schools, about MBAs and case studies and growth frameworks. And I'm sure there's value there. But me? I learned the fundamentals of leadership, operations, and innovation with headphones in, reading the *The Handbook of Applied Cryptography* in the back of a Texas high school classroom, writing eggdrop scripts while pretending to do my homework.

And I still think that was the best damn early education I could've ever asked for.

CHAPTER 3: DONUTS, DONGLES, AND DROPOUTS

While I was spending my nights lost in the digital ether of IRC channels and reverse-engineering software, my days—and many of my nights—were just as wild. My world wasn't just about cracking code; it was about running with a crew of friends we called the GWC, the "Ghetto Whip Crew." The name was a loving homage to my car: a beat-up, brown, 1988 Plymouth Colt station wagon with fake wood paneling. It was a truly terrible car, but it was all I had.

See, two weeks after my parents bought me my first car, a sporty used red Geo Storm, I totaled it by plowing it straight into the back of a friend's Ford Bronco. My parents, understandably pissed, were not taking any more chances. They gave me a budget of $400 for the next car. The Ghetto Whip was the result.

GWC was my tribe. My friend Jonathon Brown was a de facto leader, a kleptomaniac with a heart of gold who could walk into any gas station and emerge with four bottles of Boone's Strawberry Hill wine cooler tucked into his pants. It wasn't great, but for a bunch of 15-to-18-year-olds, it did the job. Our weekends were a blur of field parties, late-night tubing trips on the Comal and Guadalupe rivers, and taking over the house of anyone whose parents were out of town.

One afternoon, a buddy and I decided to try out a new steamroller bong—a long, horizontal PVC pipe, open on one end, with a makeshift cutout on top for a glass bowl. We parked the Ghetto Whip near the river and proceeded to smog the car out completely. I was obliterated. I mumble-giggled to my friend to put the bong back in its stash spot under the seat. He didn't. I dropped him off and somehow managed to pilot the station wagon home, where I made a beeline for the couch and crashed hard.

I woke up an hour later to my dad standing over me, holding the massive steamroller. "What the heck is this, Ryan?!" he yelled. Busted. He had come home, seen me passed out and reeking of pot, went to my car and glanced in my car window where he saw the bong sitting in plain sight on the back seat. Life would never be the same after that.

The real trouble started when my parents, still furious about the steamroller bong incident, went to my public high school to pull me out as punishment. The administration was confused. "Ryan?" they said, "He hasn't been showing up for weeks." They told my parents they had tried to call, but they could never get ahold of anyone. That's because I had used my burgeoning tech skills to put the school's lone outbound number on call block. My parents were livid and, now, deeply embarrassed.

Their solution was to enroll me in our church's tiny high school, Dayspring Christian Academy, which had about 10 students. The thinking was that with such a small group, there was no way for me to disappear. I couldn't hide, but I could still hack.

The school was obsessed with the computer lab games that came pre-installed on all the Windows machines, especially Pinball and Minesweeper. It was their primary form of entertainment. After a few days of giving it a try, I had legitimately made the top 3 on the Pinball high-score list. But then I had an idea. An impulse. What if I just reversed the executable files for the games, found where the high scores were stored, and put my name at the top of everything?

I went home that night, opened pinball.exe in a disassembler, and started poking around. I found the strings and almost immediately located the Windows Registry key where the data was stored: HKEY_CURRENT_USER\Software\Microsoft\Plus!\Pinball. I pulled it up in the registry editor and there it was: a list of the top ten names and their high scores, completely unencrypted. It was too easy.

I wrote a simple batch script to reset all ten spots on the leaderboard. The new champion for every single high score would be "RyanRocks," with the unbeatable score of nine hundred and ninety-nine trillion. I took the script to school on a diskette and waited until everyone was in chapel. While they were praying, I snuck into the empty computer lab and, one by one, inserted the diskette into every machine and double clicked the file. Boom. Five minutes later, the operation was complete.

Let's just say I severely underestimated the response. This wasn't a harmless prank to them; it was a violation. Kids were legitimately ready to get violent over it. One student was visibly crying as he walked out of the lab that day, his hard won Pinball glory erased.

Many times in my life my jokes didn't land, and this was a spectacular example. It was a massive miscalculation of social dynamics.

The school asked me to leave shortly after that. My parents were absolutely embarrassed and crushed. I wasn't just a truant anymore; I was a digital vandal who made another kid cry. After that, I was officially done with the charade of formal education. I walked into a testing center, took my GED cold, and finished high school on my own terms.

The parties, however, only escalated. One weekend, my parents went to the East Coast for a work trip, and I planned a huge blowout at our house. Around 9 p.m., as things were getting going, a convoy of cars pulled up. It was my older brother, Matt, who was 19 at the time. "Matt? What are you doing here?" I asked. "I'm throwing a party," he said. "Get the fuck out of here." "Bro, you don't even live here, and we're already having a party!" Before things could get ugly, Mikey, Matt's best friend and someone who's always been like a big brother to me, stepped in. "Nah, it's cool," he mediated. "You guys just stay on the back porch, we'll be on the front porch, and we'll share the kitchen."

So that's what we did. For about two hours, it was wild, two parties coexisting in chaotic harmony. Then we got the knock. Not the cops. It was Jonathon's parents, there to get his little sister who had no business being there. They stormed in, grabbed her by the hair mid-swing of a Natural Light, and dragged her outside. "Get your fucking ass in the truck, now!" her dad yelled. "And you, Ryan, this is not the last you will hear from us!" As I walked back in the house, a friend pointed out, "Hey Ryan, you still have that joint behind your ear!" Oops.

Twenty minutes later, more headlights. This time, it was the cops. People scattered into the woods in every direction. I answered the door. The officers were surprisingly cool. They'd received a report about underage drinking and just told us to shut it down. If they got called back, we'd all be cited. Most people left, including Matt and his crew. My friends and I, however, stayed up late, got way too intoxicated, and started jumping off the second-story balcony onto the living room couches below.

It wasn't all chaos. Across the street from Jonathon's house was a massive water tower on a ridge overlooking the entire city. Climbing it was a rite of passage for our crew. It was terrifying, scaling that ladder late at night, but once you got to the top, the view was breathtaking. We'd just sit up there for hours, staring at the city lights, feeling like we were on top of the world.

But we weren't on top of the world. We were teenagers in Texas, operating by a fierce, often foolish code of honor, and that world had a way of pulling you back down to earth with brutal speed. My role as GWC's de facto leader came with an unspoken rule: if you were my friend, I had your back. Period.

This was especially true for my friend we'll call Eddie to respect their privacy. In the rigid social caste system of high school, where I was often a loner, Eddie was one of the first to give me a shot. He played bass in a couple of local bands, and he invited me into his circle. That friendship was a lifeline, and my loyalty to him was absolute. One day, he came to me, furious. Some kid had keyed his blue Chevy truck over a parking spot. It was a profound violation of respect, an injustice that couldn't stand.

So I drove the Ghetto Whip to the high school parking lot with our friend Kash and one other buddy. I wasn't a student there anymore, but this was our territory. We found the kid. I didn't get out, just talked to him through my open car window. "Hey man, what's your problem? Why are you keying people's trucks?"

His response was to tell me to fuck off before throwing a sucker punch that caught me square in the face. It was pure anger and humiliation. He was the one in the wrong, and I was the one bleeding. I didn't want to fight on school property— that was a shitstorm I didn't need—so I told him we could meet elsewhere and settle it. He told me to fuck off again and sped off. But I knew where he lived.

We followed him. I parked on the street, not his property, and honked the horn. "Come outside, let's finish this." The door opened, but he wasn't alone. He was holding a rifle.

I saw his girlfriend come out behind him, trying to stop him, but he walked forcefully toward my truck, his movements stiff with determination. My blood ran cold. This wasn't a fistfight. In the split second it took to process the glint of the barrel, my brain screamed one thing: *GO*. I slammed the accelerator. As we peeled out, I saw Kash, who was on his knees in the open back of the truck, throw his arms up in pure disbelief at the kid for bringing out a gun. Then came the sharp crack of the shot. It hit the tailgate with a hard, metallic *thump*, right below where Kash was.

We were just screaming in the car. "Fuck that guy! Why would you bring a gun to a fucking fight?" Beneath the anger was the vibrating hum of pure terror. We drove to a gas station and called 911. In moments of crisis, a strange calm always descends on me. I explained the whole situation to the police. Just as I was talking, I saw the kid's car drive by. "There he goes!" The cops chased him down and brought him back to the gas station, now a chaotic swirl of flashing lights. And in the middle of it all, my older brother, Matt, drove by. He pulled over, got out, and when I explained what happened, his face shifted into a look of such fierce, protective rage that it startled me. He was ready to kill the kid for me.

My brother and I weren't close then; we had different crews and didn't talk much. But in that moment, seeing him ready to go to war for me—it was pivotal. I felt like I actually had a brother, someone who would, without hesitation, take a bullet for me. The kid got a felony for assault with a deadly weapon, but the event left a permanent mark. It was a terrifying lesson on the fragility of life and how quickly teenage dramas could escalate into something far, far darker.

But the recklessness always found its way back. One night, we were celebrating Chris Reynold's birthday at his house with a bottle of Captain Morgan rum. His mom came home early and kicked us out. We decided to make the long trip back to my house, so we all piled into my Ford Ranger. For some reason, we decided it would be hysterical to put the Captain Morgan bottle in the passenger seat with the seatbelt on. As we neared my old high school, I had an idea. It was the night before the first day of senior year for the classes I should have been in. I pulled into the front parking lot, slowly crawled my truck over the curb, and started doing donuts in the grass right in front of the school.

We were laughing hysterically until I tried to jump the curb to get out. The truck centered, stuck. We were freaking out, trying to push it off, when a cop car pulled in. "Well, what happened here, boys?" the officer asked.

"Man, am I glad to see you," I said, trying to play it cool. "We got stuck on this curb and could use some help getting off it!"

His flashlight hit the torn-up grass, then my face. "How much have you had to drink tonight?" Just as he asked, two more cop cars pulled up. It might have ended there, but when the tow truck driver arrived and flipped the front seat forward to get to the gear, there he was: the Captain, still buckled in. We couldn't help but laugh. The cops were not impressed.

They booked Johnny and me for criminal mischief. I'm still lucky I didn't get a DUI. I had to make the call to my mom from jail that night and explain everything. She was livid. Chris, the birthday boy, got let go, but with no money and no phone, he had to walk 13 miles back to his mom's house. Happy birthday, man.

That was my life then. A frantic, dual existence—one foot in the esoteric, digital world of hacking and keygens, and the other firmly planted in the muddy, beer-soaked, and often stupid reality of teenage rebellion in suburban Texas. Both were about pushing boundaries, but both were leading me down a path that was getting darker and more dangerous by the day.

CHAPTER 4:
ROCK BOTTOM

Long before the drugs, I was wrestling with a kind of internal static I couldn't silence. Social anxiety was my default setting: sweaty palms, a queasy stomach, and ragged breathing any time I had to meet someone new. Confidence felt like a foreign language.

Middle school in Texas threw fuel on that fire. First day of football practice, end of session, Coach had us take a knee. As I knelt, my entire vision went black. Panic clawed at me. "Coach, I can't see! I can't see, Coach!" I yelled. An assistant coach pulled me aside, got me water, a cold towel. But the damage was done. From then on, I was the "Coach, I can't see!" kid. Middle schoolers can be weapons-grade cruel. They nearly drove me mad with that taunt, echoing down hallways for years, a constant reminder of my perceived weakness. It still twists something in my gut today.

My weight was another battleground. I've always struggled, always been the chubby kid, and school was a minefield. I'd try to deflect with humor, wearing baggy shirts with slogans like "SPAM" plastered over a picture of the can, hoping they'd laugh at the shirt and miss the self-conscious nerd drowning in it.

Then there was Camp Capers in sixth grade, an Episcopal church camp. It should have been fun. Instead, I was relentlessly picked on, christened "Chunk" after the kid from *The Goonies*. "Do the Truffle Shuffle, Chunk!" they'd yell. Humiliation burned through me. I begged to go home, but the counselors insisted they'd "talk to the other kids." It mostly stopped, but the experience carved itself into me—a core trauma. It sucks to be the fat kid outcast. It sucks to be picked on. It sucks to be the underdog. Maybe that's why I've always fought for them when I got the chance.

My first real girlfriend, back in eighth grade, felt like an escape. We'd skip school, walk to the local bowling alley, play arcade games, smoke cigarettes, and make out in shadowy corners. Then, a few months later, she tried to take her own life while I was on the phone with her, swallowing a bottle of Tylenol. I had to hang up on her, hoping the shrill hang-up tone would be loud enough to wake her mom. It was. Her mom got her to the hospital in time.

A few weeks later, she broke up with me for some hipster kid named Mike from the same bowling alley. I was crushed, didn't understand. Later, the truth slithered out: my own older brother had made out with her when he was giving her a ride home. Cool. Fucked up. I still don't fully know how to process that, but it probably explains the breakup. It's hard to stay with someone you know you're betraying.

So, when I was 17 and my childhood friend, recently moved into a shitty apartment on San Antonio's northeast side, sprinkled cocaine onto a piece of foil, lit it from beneath, and inhaled the fumes through a straw, the landscape of my mind was already pretty bleak. "Your turn," he said casually, passing it over. *Fuck it.* I took the foil and hit it.

It was the best fucking feeling in the world. Warmth rushed through my body, obliterating the relentless anxiety and self doubt, the shame of being "Chunk" and "Coach, I can't see!" For the first time ever, I felt genuinely confident and clear headed, like I was finally discovering who I was meant to be. But clarity fades. Confidence fades even faster.

Within weeks, cocaine turned into meth, weekends blurred into weekdays, and the shitty apartment became a revolving door of strangers chasing their own chemical escapes. School became irrelevant. Friends who cared started pulling away, watching me spiral further out of control. Before long, I was kicked out, alone on a dark street, shivering and fucking terrified, realizing I'd become someone completely unrecognizable—even to myself.

My parents reluctantly took me back into their house, tucked away in the middle-of-nowhere Texas Hill Country, and I started detoxing. It was absolute hell—nights drenched in sweat, body screaming for drugs, mind haunted by shame. At 18, I thought I was chasing freedom. I'd moved out, convinced I was going to live "the good life"—drinking, partying, bouncing between jobs. But the reality hit hard and fast: I wasn't living, I was drowning. I came home one night, looked my dad in the eye, and the truth spilled out: "Dad, I'm really messed up." That moment cracked something open. I'd tried doing life my way. It nearly destroyed me.

Then, one morning during detox, my mom urgently called from work. "Turn on the TV," she said breathlessly. "A plane just hit the World Trade Center!" I watched in stunned disbelief as a second plane slammed into the other tower. The world seemed to be coming unglued, mirroring the chaos inside me. I needed to do something, find some stability. Inspired by a potent mix of anger, patriotism, and a desperate need for change, I thought about joining the military – maybe fly helicopters (yeah, right, I probably would have ended up in artillery).

Instead, I started attending my parents'

church regularly. My old high school friend was the youth pastor there, and he asked if I wanted to help. Suddenly, I was immersed: Sunday services, Wednesday night youth group, Sunday youth bible study. I got heavily involved in mentorship and discipleship. It was a lifeline, a genuinely great time in my life, a flicker of hope that I could change.

My parents had been praying for me. Quietly, patiently. My dad had even started gathering materials from Oklahoma Wesleyan University, hoping I might consider a different path. Our pastor, Desi Henk, encouraged me to serve as a youth counselor at a summer camp for the Texas/Louisiana Wesleyan district—which, as fate would have it, was hosted at OKWU.

While at that camp, something stirred in me. The Dean of Student Life from OKWU, Eddie Shigley, was the speaker. One night, during a worship service, I felt an undeniable pull, a profound sense like God was telling me that Oklahoma Wesleyan was where I was supposed to be. I pulled Eddie aside, shared a condensed version of my messed-up story, and expressed my interest in the school. We prayed about it. I left that conversation feeling like I knew my next step.

When I got home from camp and was unloading my bags, I saw an information folder and pamphlet on the kitchen table. It was for Oklahoma Wesleyan University. I was astonished. I hadn't told my parents about my experience at camp or my conversation with Eddie. When I asked my Dad about it, he said he'd looked them up a few weeks prior, thinking it might be something I'd want to check out, and the info packet had simply arrived while I was gone. I got pretty emotional. It felt like a direct sign. Was God actually talking to me?

The fleeting thoughts of military enlistment faded. I immediately emailed Eddie Shigley, filled out the application, sent in my horrible transcripts, and within a few days, I was accepted on academic probation. I did it. I somehow made it to a real school. My dad's casual question, "Wanna check out Oklahoma Wesleyan University first?" which came as I was still vaguely pondering the ASVAB, wasn't so random after all. It was part of a current already pulling me in a new direction. That question, that path, changed my entire life.

PART II: THE ARENA

CHAPTER 5:

TURNING POINT

9/11 was the gut punch that forced me to seriously reconsider everything. Watching those towers crumble wasn't just shocking—it felt deeply personal, a visceral wake-up call that reverberated through every part of me.

My world had been internal chaos for so long, and suddenly here was that chaos magnified a million times over, broadcast live into every home. The adrenaline surged through me, a potent mix of anger, grief, and an urgent, almost primal desire to act. I was done being passive. I wanted to fight.

I dove into getting myself ready for enlistment with relentless determination. I started working at a white-water rafting outfit on the Guadalupe River, lugging heavy rafts around all day, fighting the currents, and spending endless hours in the scorching Texas sun. I watched the pounds melt away and felt my strength and stamina building. For the first time in years, I felt a clarity of purpose—a focus I hadn't experienced since those late nights reverse-engineering code, driven by pure obsession. The military felt like a tangible way to channel my intensity.

But then, fate pivoted—literally the day before I was set to take the ASVAB, as I was still mentally preparing for that path, my dad strolled into the room with that quiet, almost casual offer: "Wanna check out Oklahoma Wesleyan University first?"

College? Really? The idea was almost laughable. The last time I'd set foot in a traditional classroom setting, I got expelled for being "too influential" on kids half my age and hacking the Pinball high-scores. I had a GED, a history of addiction, and a rap sheet of digital mischief. I wasn't exactly what you'd call prime college material. But something about my dad's voice, and the almost surreal way the OKWU pamphlet had appeared after my experience at the youth camp, made me stop and think. Maybe this was one of those moments you don't argue with.

So, we drove up to Bartlesville, Oklahoma. And I'm not gonna lie—I was skeptical as hell. I pictured a stuffy, judgmental environment. But something shifted the moment I stepped onto the OKWU campus. It wasn't the architecture or the course catalog. It was the people. The energy. There was an almost palpable sense of belonging. I'd spent so much of my life feeling like an outsider, the "Chunk" or the "Coach, I can't see!" kid, the troublemaker. Here, I didn't feel judged. I felt... welcomed. It was a stark contrast to every other educational institution I'd ever encountered. That seed planted at the summer youth camp—the encounter with Eddie Shigley, the feeling of a divine nudge, the admissions staffer who'd told me flat-out, "We can make this happen, GED or not"—began to sprout.

I was admitted on academic probation. I had to prove I could keep my grades up. It felt like a test—one last shot to prove that all my chaotic energy could be channeled into something productive. And so, I did. I started working multiple jobs on the side to pay my way—everything from web design for local businesses to random odd jobs.

Of course, old habits die hard. The allure of that fiber internet in the dorms was too much to resist. My early hacking skills found a new playground. I was downloading terabytes of movies and shows from private FTP sites, often in exchange for uploading music rips I'd sourced. My traffic was colossal, easily ten times what the IT department was flagging from students using torrents. But since all my downloads came from what looked like a single IP address (likely a bouncer, a compromised server acting as a relay), it didn't fit the pattern of peer-to-peer traffic. The IT team was stumped. They'd block a handful of torrenters daily, but my massive data stream just kept flowing.

When questioned, I'd innocently tell them I was video chatting extensively with my "girlfriend in Europe." They even raided my computer a few times, but I had a hidden profile for all my... extracurricular digital activities. They never found a thing. (Sorry, OKWU IT team!) It was a reminder that even in this new environment, a part of me still thrived on outsmarting systems.

I kept my head down academically and stayed hungry. But at one point, I seriously thought about walking away. The structure felt confining, and I'd landed a decent job offer. Why stick around and finish school when I could already be earning?

That's when one of my professors, Dr. David Cochran, pulled me aside. He was different. He had a highly analytical, pragmatic intellect much like my own, but he coupled it with a deep-seated entrepreneurial spirit and an uncanny ability to cut through the bullshit. He didn't scold or lecture. He just had this way of seeing the best in people, of unearthing their true motivation and using it to push them. He asked me a question that changed everything:

"What do YOU want to learn?"

I rattled off a list of advanced programming topics, cybersecurity concepts, and emerging web technologies that weren't part of the standard curriculum. Without hesitation, he helped me build a custom curriculum through directed study, allowing me to chase my passions while staying enrolled. His belief in me was a lifeline.

That trust culminated in my senior capstone project. It was Dr. Cochran's brainchild: a website called volunteerbartlesville.net. The goal was to create a central hub for all the non-profits in Bartlesville, allowing them to post volunteer opportunities that community members could easily find and sign up for. Before this, I was a coder, plain and simple. I lived in the terminal. But this project threw me into a new role. Dr. Cochran had me sitting in meetings with the local United Way, listening to their needs, hearing the problems they were having. For the first time, I wasn't just translating a command into code; I was translating a human problem into a technical solution. I was becoming a product manager.

I built it from the ground up using PHP and a MySQL database, but the real prize for me was getting to use Ajax. At the time, Ajax was revolutionary—it was the magic that allowed web pages to update content without a full page refresh, making them feel fast and dynamic like a desktop application. I was obsessed with learning it. This project was my excuse.

Dr. Cochran was the perfect mentor through it all. He had this incredible patience, guiding me on everything from sanitizing database inputs to designing user-friendly forms. But he also knew when to step back and let me build. He had this uncanny ability to meet you on your level, to strip away the formal bullshit of the professor-student dynamic. It never felt like a boss-subordinate relationship; it felt like a friendship. He was teaching us how the world worked. He invited us to his house for dinner. We met his wife and his kids, who were just little guys back then. He didn't just teach me code; he showed me a blueprint for a different kind of life, one where professional respect and genuine personal connection could coexist. I was rough around the edges before college, and so much of my maturation—the way I learned to talk to customers, send a professional email, and just carry myself—I owe to his influence. He was instrumental.

It was also around this time, during orientation week, that I met Jenn. We were in line, and she was joking with a friend about wanting a toe-ring tattoo. I turned and deadpanned, "You should try a Sharpie first. Less painful. You can test out a few designs." She laughed. We started dating soon after. And that was it—another one of those seemingly small moments I didn't fully understand the weight of until much later.

Choosing OKWU over enlistment, choosing to stay when I could have dropped out, choosing to learn from a mentor who saw me as more than just a student—these decisions fundamentally altered the course of my entire life. I went from spiraling to grounded. From broken to rebuilding. From a GED dropout haunted by past failures to a college student with a future. It didn't matter that my journey looked different from everyone else's. I was finally on one that was going somewhere.

And for the first time in a long, long time, I wasn't running away from something. I was running toward it.

CHAPTER 5.5: THE SHORTEST JOB I EVER HAD

Bartlesville, Oklahoma, is the kind of place where the Walmart feels like downtown, and if you hit a red light, you must've taken a wrong turn. It's a town where a single Starbucks opening made the front page of the Examiner-Enterprise, the local newspaper. Summers stretched out like the cracked pavement on Nowata Road, hot and slow, unless you were in a band or on the church drama team. I wasn't in either. A lot of my friends were in Reckless Hope, a Christian alt-rock band with dreams bigger than the gas money they had. They all lived in the same shitty 2-story apartment complex with cinderblock walls and air conditioning units that sounded like jet engines but barely worked.

It was the summer after my first year at Oklahoma Wesleyan. I didn't have a plan, and I definitely didn't have money. Josh Howard, the drummer for Reckless Hope and a good friend, told me they were all working at this telemarketing company over on the edge of town, and they were hiring. I was skeptical until he said, "They give you one of those huge insulated 32oz mugs."

Sold.

I don't remember the interview process—maybe there wasn't one. But I got the job. They handed me that glorious chunk of plastic like it was a company badge. White with blue lettering, sweating ice water just as I imagined it would. I felt employed. A man with purpose.

Monday rolled around, and Nick Messer, a good friend and bassist of Reckless Hope, and I showed up together for orientation. The building was a tan stucco box with windows so tinted you couldn't see the despair inside. The training room smelled like carpet glue and body spray. We were seated in rows facing away from our computers. No touching. Just a 30-page onboarding document filled with the kind of legalese and "company values" slides designed to murder neurons.

Day two, they let us power on the machines. Windows 98 flickered to life. The monitors hummed with static, the screen showing some login screen for a dialer app. Still, no touching. Just more waiting, reading, and squirming in ergonomic chairs made of betrayal.

But me? I've always been curious. Restless. Wired to break things just to see how they work. I leaned over to Nick.

"Watch this," I whispered, suppressing a grin.

I popped open the command prompt, black screen blinking like a dare. Then:

net send * "sup dog :P"

Enter.

The entire room erupted in simultaneous "DING!" sounds as 20-plus computers received the message. sup dog :P. Message box, front and center. Josh started laughing so hard he doubled over. A few others chuckled. I felt like I'd just dropped the hottest mixtape in Bartlesville.

Then... *ping*.

Another box appeared on my screen:

who is this?

Another:

stay where u are.

Shit.

Turns out this place wasn't just one office. It was part of a massive franchise operation. Over 2,000 computers on the same flat subnet. Every. Single. One. Got my little joke.

My stomach dropped. Palms slick. Suddenly the air felt thick, like I was breathing through a wet sock.

Ten minutes later, two guys with clipboards entered the room like secret police. "Just checking machines," they said, eyes scanning serial ports like bounty hunters. They started at the far end. I turned to Nick.

"I'm about to get fired. Uh oh."

He blinked at me. "Wait—you did that?!"

As they closed in, I began packing my backpack.

They reached my desk. One looked at the machine, then at me, then back again. "Get your stuff and come with us."

"Already packed," I said, standing like I was expecting the call. They walked me down a carpeted hallway that stretched like a slow-motion plank. We passed gray cubicles where actual employees wore headsets and tried to sell credit repair services to people who couldn't afford cereal.

We arrived at the manager's office. A corner room. Closed door. Smelled like Arby's and frustration. Behind the desk was a large man with a bristled beard, cheap loafers, and the sweaty menace of someone who never had a dream, just promotions.

He didn't say hello.

"You know what you did was a felony?!"

"Uh, I just typed net sen—"

"No. You hacked our systems. The CEO got your message!" I blinked. The message? The one that said sup dog :P?

"You're lucky we don't press charges. I convinced them you were just a dumb kid. Now get the hell out. You're fired."

And just like that, I was.

They walked me to the exit, one guy on each side like I might try to shoulder-roll into the server room on the way out. As we approached the front, I remembered something.

"Hey… I left my mug back in the training room. Can I grab it?"

"No," one said flatly, opening the door.

The door shut behind me. The Oklahoma sun hit my face like a slap.

And that was the shortest job I ever had.

CHAPTER 6: THE POP

College was supposed to be a place for open minds, free speech, and bold ideas—or at least that's what Jenn and I thought. At Oklahoma Wesleyan University, a small, conservative Christian institution, the reality often felt different. There was a palpable undercurrent of control, a sense that certain conversations were off-limits, and that genuine, critical dialogue about campus policies or broader societal issues was subtly (and sometimes not-so-subtly) discouraged. We both found ourselves increasingly frustrated by what felt like an administration more interested in maintaining a particular image than fostering true intellectual exploration.

Out of this frustration, Jenn and I decided to create something entirely our own, something that would pry open the closed doors of campus discourse. We called it "The POP"—short for "Point of Perspective"—an anonymous newspaper and accompanying web forum dedicated to open dialogue, fearless debate, and unapologetic truth. It was, in essence, Reddit before Reddit existed, conceived as a digital and physical haven where ideas and opinions could thrive without fear of retribution or censorship.

Launching "The POP" was exhilarating, a taste of pure, unfiltered entrepreneurial adrenaline mixed with a dash of subversive thrill. We designed and wrote the content in secret. For the first print issue, Jenn and I worked like clandestine operatives, stealthily printing copies and then, just before mealtimes when the cafeteria would be at its busiest, scattering them across tables to ensure maximum visibility. We didn't stop there. We went further, boldly chalking the URL for the web forum on sidewalks and walls around campus, a guerrilla marketing campaign daring students to log on and speak out.

The response was immediate and overwhelming. It was like uncorking a shaken bottle. Students eagerly dove into passionate discussions and fierce debates, openly critiquing school policies, sharing honest reflections on campus life, and exploring topics that would never have seen the light of day in official channels. The forum buzzed with activity. Anonymous articles submitted to us for print were raw, sometimes funny, often sharply critical, but always authentic. It was everything we'd envisioned—a vibrant, student-driven space that felt powerful and essential.

But that kind of authentic power rarely goes unnoticed by those who prefer the status quo. The excitement quickly drew the attention of the administration. Jenn, who held the prestigious Eagle Scholarship which covered nearly all her tuition, soon became the visible target. The University President at the time, since retired, called her on the phone that summer. I wasn't on the call, but I felt the weight of it, the anxiety radiating off Jenn before and the quiet devastation after. From what I understood, a tense confrontation unfolded. The President made it unequivocally clear that her scholarship —and her future at the school—hung precariously in the balance. She was cornered, forced to choose between our passionate pursuit of free speech and her educational and financial security.

Under immense pressure, Jenn made the agonizing decision. "The POP" was to be shut down. It was a deeply painful concession, a compromise that I know weighed heavily on her and felt like a betrayal of the very principles we were championing. For me, it was a bitter pill, a harsh lesson in the realities of institutional power versus idealistic conviction.

It wasn't merely about censorship; it felt like a profound disappointment, a moment where the university, in my eyes, failed to live up to what a true academic environment should be.

I remember talking to Dr. Cochran about it all. He had been the professor who saw potential in me, who helped keep me in school when I was on the edge of dropping out. And here we were again, facing a different kind of challenge, one that threatened my belief in the institution itself. He didn't condone what happened, nor did he criticize the administration directly to me.

Instead, he listened. He helped me process my anger and disillusionment by reframing it as a learning experience, however harsh. He reminded me that intellectual courage often comes with a cost, and that learning wasn't about blind obedience but about developing critical thinking, even when it led to uncomfortable truths or friction with authority. His steady mentorship helped me make sense of the experience without becoming completely cynical.

Though silenced prematurely, "The POP" was undeniably ahead of its time. It laid the groundwork for the type of open, digital dialogues that would later define platforms like Reddit, which I'd ironically play a part in years later. This experience wasn't just a defeat—it was a profound lesson in bravery, resilience, and the very real cost of standing firmly by one's principles, especially when faced with disproportionate power.

Looking back, I realize how pivotal this chapter was. "The POP" planted seeds that shaped my future decisions and my unwavering commitment to championing free expression, authenticity, and transparency in every venture that followed. The voice we sparked, however briefly, at Oklahoma Wesleyan echoed onward, influencing the paths Jenn and I would take, and forever altering my views on courage, community, and the transformative, sometimes disruptive, power of speaking one's truth.

CHAPTER 7: THE GOLDEN TICKET

After the fallout from "The POP," Jenn and I knew our time at OKWU was drawing to a close. The place had undeniably shaped us, providing a crucible for growth and a soft place to land when I was rebuilding. But it had also shown us the limits of its walls. I was restless, my brain buzzing with ideas that felt too big for Bartlesville. Oklahoma had been a necessary sanctuary for healing and rediscovery, but it wasn't where my story was going to peak. I was ready to build, to take what I'd learned and apply it on a bigger stage.

During my final semesters, I threw myself into side projects. One of them—a music review website TheBeep dot net — started as a fun way to blend my interests in tech and culture. It gained unexpected traction. Record labels noticed and started sending boxes of unreleased albums, eager for exposure on the platform. I recruited English majors to write reviews, paying them in CDs – a currency they gladly accepted. Behind the scenes, the old hacker in me was still very much alive. I'd quietly make perfect digital rips of these pre-release albums and share them with my old IRC contacts. It was still me, still testing boundaries, still finding ways to distribute content, but now it felt less like rebellion and more like an early, unrefined form of guerilla marketing and community building. It had a nascent purpose.

Then came the weekend that literally changed my life. Facebook had just launched its developer platform. It was a Friday afternoon, the campus was quiet, and I decided to see what this new platform was all about.

I cobbled together a simple app that pulled headlines from TechCrunch. It took a few hours, nothing too complex. On a whim, I found Michael Arrington's email address and cold-emailed him, the founder of TechCrunch, with a brief description and a link. I didn't expect much. To my astonishment, within hours, he emailed back. We jumped on a Skype call. I pitched the app, my voice probably cracking with a mixture of nerves and excitement. He loved it. He immediately saw the potential.

That weekend, everything exploded. Arrington blogged about the app. By Monday, when I showed up for my part-time job at PDG+creative, a local marketing agency, the owner, Matt, told me the company voicemail box was full. *The New York Times*, MSNBC, AOL, MTV—everyone, it seemed, wanted their own Facebook app. PDG+creative transformed into a leading Facebook development shop almost overnight, with me at the center of this whirlwind. The Facebook Platform team even took notice and invited me to be part of their early developer community.

I saw a massive window of opportunity. I proposed to Matt that we go all-in, open a San Francisco office, and really capitalize on this momentum. But Matt, to his credit, was honest—he was a small business owner in Oklahoma, and that kind of leap, that kind of risk, wasn't in his DNA. I respected his position. But I also knew, with a certainty that settled deep in my bones, that I couldn't stay. My path was pointing west.

So I started interviewing remotely. I soon found myself in the running with two incredible, but very different, companies. One was ZURB, a world-renowned UX and UI design agency in San Jose. The other was DotSpotter, a scrappy, early-stage startup based in Berkeley, CA.

I cold emailed DotSpotter after reading a job posting for a Senior Designer position. Here's that e-mail verbatim, with all the mistakes kept.

Original Message

From: James Ryan Merket
Sent: Tuesday, November 6, 2007 9:27am
To: jobs@dotspotter.com

Subject: Front-end XHTML/CSS Guru

Good Morning,

My name is Ryan Merket, and I am a 25 year old Interactive Creative currently employed for a creative agency in the midwest called PDG +creative.

Let me tell you little bit about myself, I have spent the last 3 years completing my Visual Communication degree and working full-time at PDG+creative. I recently accepted PDG's proposal of promoting me to Creative Director, but my heart lies in the bay area. I can't stop thinking about being out there, and working with a company about revolutionize the way people use the internet (that's you).

I recently married my college sweetheart on October 6th, and soon my wife and I will be packing our bags and headed to San Francisco. She would like to attend Stanford and receive her Masters, and I will be looking for a company to continue my career with.

I love design, especially interactive design. I am a sucker for beautiful typography, and have been known to take screenshots of well designed sites (nerd, I know). I am extremely comfortable designing websites from scratch in Photoshop, and would even consider my XHTML/CSS (table less) one of my strongest assets. I am a big fan of integrating web standards in all of my projects, whether that be a Flash site, huge dynamically driven site, or small HTML site.

Just like everyone else, I am a huge fan of AJAX, and love implementing it into my projects. But I also make sure all my JavaScript is degradable and doesn't break the website if the user has JavaScript turned off. I believe usability is a huge part of web design, and even suggest usability studies on all projects.

Though design and front-end would be my "bread and butter", I am also pretty comfortable hand coding PHP and MySQL. I helped develop a CMS called Caffeine for my present employer. It includes an extremely intuitive interface with drag-n-drop functionality.

I work well under pressure, and have been accustomed to high work loads, and unbelievable stress levels — but it would be nice to have the culture and atmosphere of the bay area to help me unwind.

Take a look at my portfolio: www.ryanmerket.com

And download my resume: www.ryanmerket.com/resume.pdf

So, where do I sit? :)

Ryan Merket

ryan@xxxxxxx.com

555-555-1212

Norbert, the co-founder and CTO of Dotspotter, emailed me back at 6pm CT and said he liked my portfolio but wanted to see if I could convert one of Kris's Photoshop designs on the new Dotspotter homepage, and convert it to HTML/CSS. I love challenges like this.

Instead of going home from the office at 6pm and working on the challenge tomorrow, I turn my PC back on and got it to work. I might have grabbed a Subway sandwhich or something, but I cranked, hard. I typed out, by hand, the entire HTML/CSS for that design in Firefox and Chrome, and even had it working for IE7. Within a few hours, I responded to Norbert and Kris's challenge...

Norbert,
Please take a look:

http://ryanmerket.com/ui-challenge/

Disclaimer: Developed for Firefox, looks
almost perfect in IE 7, and needs major love in IE6 (I
am very comfortable doing that too). It is getting pretty
late over here, but more than willing to make it cross
browser compliant if you would like to see me do that as
well.

I will be available at 5:00pm CST tomorrow to
discuss. Thanks again!
Ryan

Later that week, while I was in San Jose, CA to interview with ZURB, Kris emailed me again. "Hey, I saw you're in town," he wrote. "Want to grab coffee tomorrow?" I told him I was unfortunately flying out the next morning.

His response came quickly: "Oh, where are you staying? Do you mind if we come have a drink with you in the lobby tonight?"

It was already 9 p.m. I was exhausted, but I said yes. Around 9:40, the DotSpotter leadership team rolled into my hotel lobby: Kris, Norbert, the CEO Anthony Soohoo, and Jeff Clark, another leader at the company. We chopped it up for about half an hour before most of them left. Kris and I stayed and talked for another thirty minutes. It was a whirlwind meeting fueled by adrenaline and possibility.

The next day, I had two offers. The offer from DotSpotter was for twice the salary that ZURB had offered. I loved ZURB and their reputation, but the chance to get in on the ground floor of a startup, with that kind of validation from people I instantly clicked with, was too compelling to pass up. Plus they offered to double whatever ZURB offered. That helps.

I took the DotSpotter offer. The connection with that team proved to be a lasting one. Anthony Soohoo, who would later become the CEO of MoneyGram International, was instrumental in my early career and even became an angel investor in my first startup.

The team's welcoming spirit started before we even officially arrived. A few weeks before our move, Norbert met Jenn and me for breakfast in Berkeley, sketching out neighborhoods on a napkin and helping us get a lay of the land. It was an act of

kindness that went far beyond any typical hiring process.

Moving to the Bay Area was still a massive culture shock. The traffic, the sheer number of people, the honking cars—it was a lot for a kid from Texas and Oklahoma. This is where my first true mentor on the ground, Jonah Schwartz, the senior engineer at DotSpotter, became my guide. Jonah is an amazing person. He took me under his wing, patiently re-teaching me programming fundamentals from a professional perspective, a world away from my self-taught methods. He showed me how Silicon Valley engineering teams *really* work. He was kind, incredibly smart, and welcoming. We came from completely different worlds—me, a WASP from Texas, and him, a Jewish kid from Berkeley—but we connected instantly.

Those early days at DotSpotter, the people I met there like Jonah, Kris, Norbert, Jeff, Bart, and Anthony, laid the foundation for my entire career in the Bay Area. They believed in me, took a chance on me, and taught me the ropes. I had my golden ticket, and I was finally in the game.

After getting the offer from DotSpotter, Jenn and I packed up everything we owned. It wasn't much—some savings, a mattress, our beat-up 2000 Saturn, and a whole hell of a lot of hope. Leaving Oklahoma felt like stepping off a cliff. It was terrifying and exhilarating in equal measure, the first time in my life I was truly jumping without any safety net.

San Francisco hit like a tidal wave. The pace, the people, the sheer density of ambition—it was everything I had dreamed of and more. My first role there evolved quickly, and I found myself sinking deeper into product strategy and platform development. And then, in 2010, came our own big break: TechCrunch Disrupt.

While the saga of "The POP" had shown me the limits of my environment in Oklahoma, my part-time job at PDG+creative, a local marketing agency, showed me the joys of a great work culture. The owner, Matt Pendergraff, had given me a shot when I was just a college kid. He'd taught a branding class I took at OKWU, and on the last day, in front of everyone, he offered me a job. "Heck yes!" was my immediate reply.

Working with Matt was a blast. He was fun, creative, and fostered an electric atmosphere. I remember him hiding behind the 16-foot curtains in our office to jump out and scare a new hire half to death during his interview. We went from building e-commerce sites for candle makers to landing deals with AOL and MTV. If I wasn't so restless, so possessed by a gravitational pull towards something bigger, I could have happily seen myself working with Matt for years.

The pull towards San Francisco, however, was growing stronger, thanks in large part to another key mentor who entered my life: Ellen Petry Leanse. I was introduced to her through the legendary tech evangelist Guy Kawasaki.

Ellen was an early Apple employee, someone who had worked alongside Steve Jobs and his leadership team. She is a true visionary, and when she learned about the newly launched Facebook Platform, she immediately saw its world-changing potential. We connected instantly, talking for hours over the phone—me in a quiet office in Bartlesville, Oklahoma, and her in the heart of Palo Alto, CA.

She saw something in me, and her encouragement was the final push I needed. She gave me the courage, telling me plainly that I would fit in, that I could do it, that I belonged there. Together, we built a badass Facebook app called "Lists," which allowed users to create collaborative social lists, assign responsibilities, and comment on items.

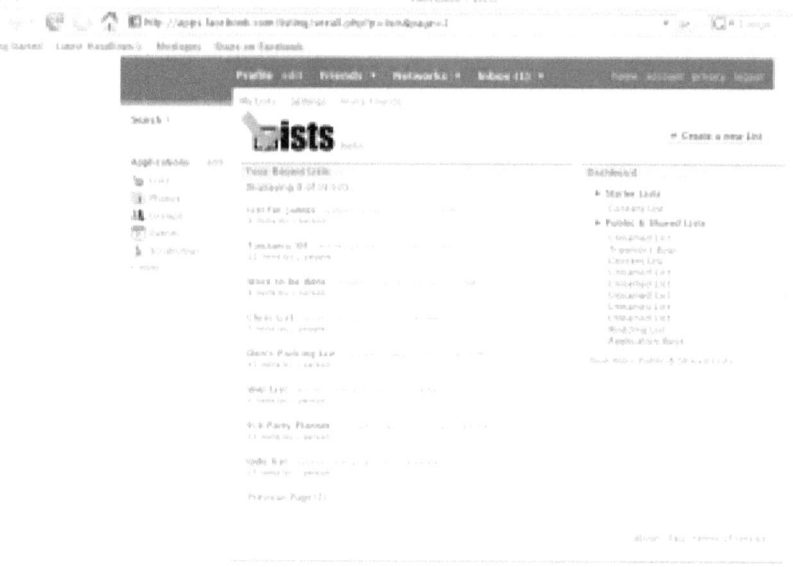

Screenshot of the Lists app within the Facebook app canvas.

We meticulously crafted our UI to seamlessly integrate with Facebook's so it felt like a native, integrated product. It was beautiful and, frankly, years ahead of its time. While it caught on well, especially in AUS/NZ, ongoing changes made to the Facebook platform focused on games and viral sheep-throwing apps instead of real world utility apps, the only option was to shut the app down. But the experience of building it with Ellen solidified my resolve. I was going to the Bay Area.

CHAPTER 8: THE BETRAYAL

My job at DotSpotter was my golden ticket into the Bay Area, but the entrepreneurial fire that had been stoked at OKWU was burning hotter than ever. Back at PDG+creative in Oklahoma before I moved to Berkeley, we had built apps for all kinds of companies. One of them was a fast-growing, venture-backed darling out of London called SpinVox, which had cool technology to convert voice to text. We built them a Facebook integration that allowed users to update their status by calling a toll-free number. It got huge coverage in TechCrunch and was a massive success.

That project planted a seed. Before we started, I had hired a talented developer from Tulsa to help with the influx of work. One day, I was walking by his desk and the idea hit me with the force of a lightning strike. "I got it," I said. "What if we did what we built for SpinVox, but for every social network? You could post from anything—phone, SMS, email, an API— and it would blast your update to all your networks at once." He loved it. I bought the domain Ping.fm, sketched out the first branding, and designed the admin dashboard, all while Jenn and I were in the middle of getting married and planning our move to California. By the time I arrived in the Bay Area, we were ready to launch.

I brought in my new friend from DotSpotter, Duncan Winter, who was the Product Manager there. Hailing from Vashon Island near Seattle, he was also relatively new to the Bay Area. I thought he would be the perfect cat herder for the team, managing the product while I focused on investors, marketing, and the front-end. At the time, the cool way to launch was with invite codes to create scarcity and buzz. So that's what we did. We launched on a Monday to a handful of friends. On Tuesday, I sent an email to Mashable, offering them an exclusive invite code for their readers.

They loved it, we set up the code "mashable" for 500 users, and they ran the story. We went viral. In two days, we had nearly 50,000 users.

A few days later, on a Saturday night, I was scrolling through Twitter when I saw a tweet from Kevin Rose, the founder of Digg and a tech celebrity at the time: "wine party with Gary V… call Scoble if you want in…" He listed a phone number. I texted it immediately: "Myself and +1 will be there." Just then, Jenn got home. "Hey honey," I said, my heart pounding, "you wanna go to a wine party?" She shrugged, "Uh, I guess?"

We jumped in our beat-up 2002 green Saturn and drove from our apartment in Berkeley to Santa Rosa. I was still deathly afraid of driving in San Francisco, so this felt like a monumental journey. We'd never even been to wine country. But I was determined to meet these tech luminaries and show them what I was building.

We found the house, a rager in full swing. We walked in and were immediately greeted by strangers and offered wine. I could smell the familiar scent of pot from the backyard. Jenn, ever the social one, started chatting about wine with a group of Gary Vaynerchuk's followers. I was on a mission, stalking Kevin Rose. That's when I saw a face I recognized but had never met: Robert Scoble, a legendary tech blogger. He was near his laptop, so I walked over.

"Hey, Scoble!" I said. "Hey man!" he replied with a huge, gregarious smile, a few glasses of wine in. "My name is Ryan Merket, and my friends and I just built Ping.fm. It lets you blast your status updates to all your social networks from anywhere in the world, even a text message!" "Oh cool! What's it called again?" he yelled over the music. "Ping dot fm! Here, use this code to sign up: RYAN40. Feel free to share it!"

Just then, Kevin Rose walked in. I quickly introduced myself and pitched him. He seemed interested. That night, I got five huge tech influencers to sign up. I was riding an incredible high. The next week, TechCrunch covered us, then VentureBeat. It was a dream come true. I did it. I came to Silicon Valley, created a product people wanted, and was off to the races.

We started looking for investors. I combed through our user database, looking for people with three-letter email domains— a trend for VCs at the time—and started cold-emailing them, thanking them for signing up and asking for a meeting. One of them, a VC out of Atlanta, was interested in investing $100,000. He asked if we had our corporation paperwork.

Uh, no?

We got off the call, and I agreed that my partner still in Tulsa would handle the legal paperwork. In the meantime, Duncan and I would keep meeting with investors and working on the product roadmap. A week later, he sent me the incorporation documents to sign. I read through them and my stomach dropped. The paperwork listed me as an employee, not a founder. I would have no board seat and would vest common shares just like any other early employee.

I was stumped. This couldn't be right. It was my idea. I got the team together. I bought the domain. I designed the product. I orchestrated the viral launch. What the heck?

I called him. He said that since he and his friend in Tulsa did the backend coding, they should be the co-founders. I would be an employee with no real say. It felt like a profound betrayal. It was clear that in any future disagreement, they could just push me out and split my shares. How could they do this? I called the Atlanta VC, explained the situation, and told him that I couldn't in good conscience do business with people I couldn't trust. I was stepping away. So that's what I did. I walked away from my own creation.

They went on to raise money from the legendary Reid Hoffman, the founder of LinkedIn. A couple of years later, in 2010, they were acquired by Seesmic.

I remember walking into the Facebook office one day and a few people yelled, "Hey, congrats!" "Huh? For what?" "You sold Ping.fm! I saw the TechCrunch article!" "Oh, thanks!" I said, my voice hollow. I walked to my desk and pulled up the announcement. The article listed the two co-founders who were joining the Seesmic team. Gutted. That should have been me. "Dude! Congrats, Merket!" someone else yelled across the hallway. "Thanks," I mumbled.

It was the weirdest, most disorienting feeling. What a fucking betrayal. It was in that moment, staring at the screen, that I decided I would leave Facebook. I would not let this be the end of my founder story.

That betrayal taught me a brutal lesson, one that has become a core part of my personal code and a pillar of the advice I give to every founder I mentor. It's about hacking the very foundation of a company to prevent it from collapsing under the weight of ambiguity. Before you build anything substantial, you must work through the formation details. You hash out the percentages, you debate the numbers, and you get it all in writing so there is no ambiguity. You make damn sure all founders have equal access to the code in a shared repo from day one.

It's a crucial piece of advice that can save a ton of heartache. I know, because I paid the tuition on that lesson so others wouldn't have to. The ghost of Ping.fm would not define me; it would fuel me. I would go out and claim the glory I felt I had rightly earned.

Three months later, I was on stage at TechCrunch Disrupt NYC 2010, launching my next startup, Appbistro.

CHAPTER 9: IMPOSTER IN PARADISE

When I joined Facebook in the spring of 2009, it felt like being issued a passport to a different dimension. This wasn't the monolithic global entity it is today; it was a sprawling, chaotic archipelago of mismatched offices in downtown Palo Alto, an organism pulsing with growth, long before the iconic "1 Hacker Way" address existed. I was recruited to the Platform team by legends like Josh Elman and Dave Morin. My mandate was intoxicating: help the world's most iconic brands—ESPN, Spotify, Disney, even The White House— weave themselves into the fabric of Facebook. On paper, it was the dream.

Inside, I was holding my breath, waiting to be found out.

Imposter syndrome is a tired phrase, but the experience is a vivid, private horror. It hit me not like a train, but like a slow moving flood, the water rising silently until I was submerged. Here I was, a high school dropout with a GED, adrift in a sea of Stanford, MIT, and Ivy League pedigrees. These people hadn't just studied the internet; in some cases, they had quite literally built its foundations. I'd walk into meetings with engineering prodigies and seasoned execs, and a single, frantic mantra would loop in my head: Today's the day they figure it out. Today's the day they realize I don't belong.

The atmosphere was a kind of controlled chaos, a whirlwind of ambition that only amplified my anxiety. Internally, it was the "serious year." Mark Zuckerberg famously wore a tie to work every day, a stark, symbolic tightening of the corporate knot. The legendary inter-office boat races and late-night drinking games were ossifying into formal policy documents and layers of approvals. I found myself wearing a sports jacket most

days, a flimsy armor of respectability, desperately trying to look the part of someone who wasn't faking it.

My job was a delicious irony. I was the bridge between Facebook and the world's top developers, debugging APIs and calming frantic partners. A former teenage keygen writer who spent years picking apart software was now an insider with commit access, checking in code to Facebook.com, helping the very kind of companies I once would have targeted.

I masked the internal flood with a dam of relentless work. I had to prove I belonged. I conceived and launched the first ever livestream event on Facebook.com—a groundbreaking series with acts like the Jonas Brothers and the Foo Fighters

that we essentially hacked together with RTMP feeds and sheer force of will. I started "Developer

Fridays," inviting top developers to campus to present their challenges directly to our engineering teams and meet Zuck. By any external metric, I was killing it. But the fun felt distant, a party I was watching through a soundproof window. The free gourmet meals, designed to keep us focused, just became another reason to stay late, another hour to feel like I was falling behind.

That immense pressure doesn't respect office walls. It's a toxic gas that seeps under the door and fills every room in your life. It followed me home to Jenn. We were newly married, still learning the complex choreography of a shared life in a new city, and the startup grind left no oxygen for us. I poured every ounce of myself into my performance at work, convinced that my worth was a currency that had to be earned, hour by hour. And it bankrupted our marriage. The space between us grew vast and silent. We argued. We cried. Eventually, shattered and exhausted, we separated.

Professionally, I was an insider at the hottest company on the planet. Personally, my most important partnership was in pieces. I was a success and a failure, all at once.

It was in the wreckage that I began to find salvation. First, with Jenn. We cautiously reconnected, talking with a raw honesty that had been suffocated by the pressure. I started therapy, fighting the ingrained belief that asking for help was an admission of weakness. Slowly, I began to excavate the years of anxiety and self-doubt.

And second, I found it in the East Bay.

While the city and the Peninsula felt like a glittering, high stakes tournament of one-upmanship, Oakland and its surroundings felt… real. It was there, away from the hum of servers and venture capital, that I built the anchor that kept me from drifting away completely. My friends there—people like Potouli Kalafanos and Karen Ting, Greg and Catrina—were artists, teachers, a chiropractor. They weren't "in tech." They were in life. With them, I wasn't "Ryan Merket, the Facebook guy." I was just Ryan.

Our rituals were antidotes to the sterile performance of my professional life. Thursday nights often meant karaoke at a dive called Mel-o-Dees in El Cerrito. The place was a glorious time capsule, with deep red felt wallpaper that seemed to absorb the joyful, off-key noise and a small room where we would dance and sing with beautiful, un-self-conscious abandon. I remember the feeling of release, laughing with Potouli over drinks while Karen and Jenn belted out some 80s anthem, the sound a chaotic, perfect symphony of not giving a damn.

They became our California family, rebuilding the sense of belonging that Jenn and I had lost. We'd go to Potouli and Karen's for a proper Greek Easter, his mom making incredible dishes and reading our fortunes from the thick sludge at the bottom of our coffee cups. We'd spend Thanksgiving at Greg and Catrina's. These weren't networking events; they were sacraments of friendship.

One of our backpacking trips became a defining metaphor for that period. Greg planned what was supposed to be a six-mile hike to Bear Lake in the Sierras. But when we arrived, the lake was crowded. Greg, ever the purist, wanted to find a more pristine spot. We kept going. And going. Twelve brutal miles later, my knee had completely given out. I was in agony,

barely able to move. For two days, I lay with my leg submerged in the ice-cold mountain lake, the glacial water a desperate attempt to bring the swelling down. We were miles from anywhere, and I was convinced they'd need a helicopter to get me out. But my friends saved me. Someone had ibuprofen. And on the long, agonizing hike out, Greg or Potouli simply took my 60-pound pack and carried it for me, leaving me free to focus on the singular, excruciating task of putting one foot in front of the other. They literally carried my weight when I couldn't.

It's a kindness that exists in a different universe from the feedback I'd one day receive from a VC that I lacked a "killer instinct." Maybe. Or maybe my instinct was just to build a human stack strong enough to carry me when the technical one inevitably crashed.

This friendship has been a constant, even through the hardest times. Watching Karen's long and brutal battle with breast cancer has been a lesson in a different kind of strength, a heartbreaking reminder of what is truly important and what is not. It's a helplessness that puts the petty anxieties of work into sharp, painful perspective.

Facebook didn't break me. It tested me, stripped me down to my foundations, and forced me to confront the imposter in the mirror. But it was in the warm, messy, karaoke-singing, mountain-hiking, food-sharing reality of the East Bay that I began to piece myself back together. I learned that strength isn't feigning invincibility. It's knowing who will carry your pack when you can no longer walk on your own. My GED wasn't a scarlet letter; it was proof of a different kind of grit. I wasn't an imposter. I was a builder. And it was time to build my own world again.

Nalin Mittal and I had co-founded a startup called Appbistro. The idea was timely and smart: an app marketplace specifically for Facebook Pages, riding the massive wave of the Facebook platform boom. We hustled hard and landed a coveted spot to launch at TechCrunch Disrupt NYC. I'd never even taken a red-eye flight before. I arrived in New York dazed, utterly sleep-deprived, and a bundle of nerves. During the on-stage rehearsal, I completely blanked on my pitch. My mind went empty. It was profoundly humiliating, standing there under the lights, unable to string words together.

When it came time for the actual launch, I stood off to the side, controlling the slides, while Nalin, ever the smooth operator, delivered the pitch. And you know what? We crushed it. The room buzzed. You could feel the energy shift. Investors leaned in. We got tough questions from some of the best in the business—Jeffrey Bussgang, Chris Fralic, Philip Kaplan. They grilled us on monetization, competition, our reliance on Facebook. We had answers. We had a plan. We had momentum.

But momentum in the startup world can be a fleeting, fickle beast. After our launch, we successfully raised $1.1 million across two funding rounds. We iterated, we learned, and eventually, we pivoted away from the Appbistro consumer marketplace and rebranded as Appstores.com—a white-label SaaS platform that allowed publishers and platforms to create their own curated app galleries. Think: ESPN launching its own branded Sports App Store. It was a smart technical move, but it split our focus. Our existing ad business, which had been gaining traction, lost momentum. Investors started getting nervous. Internally, tensions began to rise. The partnership between Nalin and I was starting to fracture under the strain.

Then came the TiE Conference. We had reserved a booth in the expo hall the year before, back when capital was flowing and optimism was high. Now, we were just months away from potentially laying everyone off. Our budget was non-existent. Still, we decided to show up. We brought a white tablecloth from home, a fishbowl to collect business cards, and my personal iMac from my desk. I loaded a Keynote presentation on a loop with our branding and product shots. It was scrappy as hell—the very definition of bootstrapping—but we were there.

As fate, or perhaps sheer dumb luck, would have it, the head of InMobi's US Business Development team walked by our booth. What we didn't know was that just days earlier, his CEO had given him a directive: find an app store company to partner with—or buy. And there we were, standing in a sea of flashy displays, with a literal sign that said: "Appstores.com."

He told us we needed to get on a call with his team in India, urgently. The very next night, we were on a Skype call with InMobi's Head of Corporate Development. The first thing he said, almost before introductions were over, was: "Don't raise your Series A. We want to buy you."

Just two days earlier, Nalin and I had gotten into a massive argument over a last-ditch plan I'd put together to try and salvage the struggling ad business. He hated it. We were on the absolute edge of collapse, both financially and as a team. A week after that Skype call, we were on a plane to Bangalore with expedited visas, pitching our hearts out to the entire InMobi executive team. It was a wild, surreal blur. And somehow, it worked.

We sold.

The acquisition wasn't a life-changing, retire-to-a-private island kind of exit. But it was a dignified one. The closing process, however, was an exercise in endurance I hadn't anticipated. InMobi decided to reincorporate in Singapore right in the middle of our deal, stretching what our US lawyers expected to be a one or two-week process into an agonizing five-month marathon. Due to the time differences with India and Singapore, late-night calls bleeding into 2 a.m. became the norm. Nalin and I made multiple trips to India to finalize terms and integration plans. It was rough. We'd been making below market salaries for years, even dropping them further towards the end just to extend our runway long enough to make this acquisition happen. The exhaustion was immense, but when the deal finally closed and a portion of the proceeds hit our accounts, the relief was palpable.

We paid our investors back. We gave our small team soft landings. We got to walk away clean, heads held high. And I walked away knowing what it feels like to stare into the abyss and then, unexpectedly, get the second chance you weren't even sure you deserved.

Sometimes, when you're absolutely certain it's over, the game throws you one more pitch. And if you're ready, if you're scrappy enough, if you refuse to quit, you might just connect. That's what this chapter of my life was: the first time I proved to myself and the world that I could build something from scratch, watch it stumble, fall down hard, and then get back up without burning everything to the ground. It wasn't a fairytale. It was a startup story. And it was mine.

CHAPTER 10: REBEL AT REDDIT

The vow I made to myself in the disorienting aftermath of my atrial fibrillation episode was absolute: I was done with the relentless travel. After fourteen trips to Bangalore in just two years, plus countless other flights for work, I had missed too much. I had a wife who needed her partner and a newborn son I desperately wanted to watch grow up. The "dream" of being a globetrotting tech executive had revealed itself to be a nightmare of missed moments and squeezing my 6′3″ frame into aluminum tubes in the sky. I promised myself I would find a job in San Francisco that mattered, one where I could make a huge impact but still be home for dinner. I had my eye on one company from the start: Reddit.

Getting a job at a place like Reddit, however, required more than just submitting a resume. I took a hacker's approach. I started digging into their public code on GitHub, identifying and reporting bugs, trying to make myself useful to the engineering team before I ever asked for anything. Then, I sent another one of those cold emails that had changed my life before. This time it was addressed to Yishan Wong and Ellen Pao, the leaders of Reddit at the time. I laid out everything I thought I could do to help them, especially around monetization, and explained why I was so passionate about their mission and community. A few weeks later, I was interviewing. A month after that, following board approval, I had an offer. My buddy Heath Black, who had helped me with my college music review site and was one of the first to help with Appbistro, was already at Reddit and put in a good word, sealing the deal.

When I walked into the office on 3rd Street, Reddit felt like the startup I'd always wanted to join. There were only about 25 people in the SF office, with another small team of 20 in Salt Lake City managing Reddit Gifts. The scale was intimate, the potential astronomical. Soon after I joined, they made the tough decision to consolidate, forcing the SLC team, including Heath, to move to San Francisco. It was bittersweet for him and his wife, Sallie, who loved Utah, but for me, it was a reunion. We were united again, hanging out on the regular.

To me, I had finally, truly made it. I'd worked at my dream company, Facebook. I'd fulfilled the founder's dream of starting a company, getting it funded, and achieving an exit. And now, here I was, on the ground floor of what I believed was the next great social network. This was success. I knew from Reddit's own blog posts that they had recently raised money at around a $50 million valuation, while only doing about $8 million a year in revenue. The math was bananas. The upside potential was staggering if they could build a real monetization engine—which was precisely the job they hired me to do. I believed in myself and what I could build, so as soon as I was able, Jenn and I took a huge leap of faith. We took $50,000 of our savings and early-exercised my employee stock options, locking in the long-term capital gains timeline. It was a massive bet, but the opportunity felt too good to be true. I even wrote a viral LinkedIn post titled "Why You Should Leave Your Job and Join Reddit Right Now," evangelizing the opportunity to everyone I knew. I was all in.

My mandate was to own and scale that nascent advertising platform. The reality, however, was that the whole system was duct-taped together with legacy code and fragile integrations. It was a one-man show, and the stakes were incredibly high.

Then the platform, and the company, were thrown into turmoil. Ellen Pao, by then interim CEO, began a necessary but hugely controversial cleanup, banning hate-filled subreddits like r/FatPeopleHate. It was the right call, but the backlash was severe. In protest, moderators shut down huge swaths of the site, causing our traffic to plummet overnight. The press had a field day. Internally, the mood was tense, the future uncertain.

It was during this chaotic period that we were deep in evaluating a strategic partnership with Google to power our ad platform. Ellen supported it; she saw a path to scale. But I saw it as a toxic deal that would betray our users' trust and privacy. Handing Google the keys felt like lighting a match inside the Library of Alexandria. I fought against it fiercely, even bringing in an ex-Google engineer to build a prototype of an in-house solution. I was overruled. The plan moved forward with a janky, embarrassing i-frame hack. I was crushed. It felt like we were sacrificing Reddit's soul for short-term revenue.

That's when everything changed again. Ellen stepped down. And in a move orchestrated by board member Sam Altman, Reddit's original co-founder, Steve Huffman, returned as CEO.

The day Steve walked back in, the vibe shifted. That night, at a celebratory dinner, he asked me what I was working on. I gave him the unvarnished truth: the Google debacle, the iframe mess, everything. When I finished, he was stunned. He leaned in and said, "Thank you for saving Reddit." It was one of the most validating moments of my career.

Things moved fast. Steve called a meeting with me and the VP of Sales. He methodically deconstructed the VP's rationale for the AdWords deal on a whiteboard until its flaws were undeniable. With that, the Google deal was dead. As we walked out, the furious VP cornered me. "Dude, what the fuck was that all about?" he demanded. "What did you say to him?!" I told him the simple truth: "He asked me what I was working on. I told him." He stormed out. The political cost of my victory was clear. In the weeks that followed, he and his top deputies stopped replying to my emails and attending my meetings. The internal environment had become untenable. It was right about then that Amazon's recruiting team contacted me. I knew it was time.

In my final months, with Steve's full backing, we did incredible work. We scrapped the iframe hack and built the foundation for Reddit's own native ad stack. We championed and launched Do Not Track (DNT) functionality, honoring user privacy despite loud objections from the sales team. And I had the honor of bringing one of Yishan Wong's brilliant ideas to life: donating 10% of Reddit's ad revenue to charities chosen by the community. We successfully distributed over $800,000 to nonprofits. It remains one of the things I'm most proud of.

Even after I left, the mutual respect with Steve remained, and I continued to help bridge the gap between Reddit's scrappy culture and its big-tech partners like AWS. Reddit was more than a job; it was a profound test of values. It was where I learned that true influence isn't about consensus—it's about conviction, and having the courage to fight for what you believe is right, no matter the personal or political cost.

CHAPTER 11: MERKET HACKS: SURVIVING THE CATHEDRAL

After the tribal, often chaotic energy of Reddit, joining Amazon Web Services was like leaving a bustling port town and entering a vast, silent cathedral built to the god of data. My role on the AWS Startup Team was designed for people like me—ex-founders who had navigated the full, dizzying arc of building and scaling, who could speak the language of panic and payroll. We were hired for our clout and empathy, but we were expected to operate with the cold, hard precision of the machine itself.

My interview with Dave Schappell, one of the team's founding members and first product manager of Amazon.com, was less a conversation than a diagnostic. "You're sharp," he said, cutting through the pleasantries, "but you need to brush up on your Leadership Principles." At Amazon, the LPs weren't motivational posters; they were scripture, the operational DNA of the company, a set of commandments we were expected to cite in our work as if defending a theological thesis.

The week-long orientation in Seattle was a full immersion baptism into this faith. On the first night, at 8

PM, our cohort of new hires was on a conference call with our leadership and the China team. One poor soul on the line was publicly, methodically eviscerated by a senior leader for using descriptive adjectives instead of quantifiable data in his update. Nobody wanted a narrative; Amazon demanded numbers. How many startups attended? What tier were they? What did the pipeline look like? Show me the data. The message was clear: anecdote was heresy.

Life inside the cathedral was governed by a relentless, metronomic rhythm. Weekly reports fed into monthly "2x2s"—concise summaries of progress and plans that were tracked in a monstrous, multi-tabbed spreadsheet. This file was a living organism that regenerated nightly on a shared drive, so arcane and complex that as a Mac user, I often had to remote into a Windows Virtual Machine just to perform the ritual of updating it. We were expected to know which cloud platform every significant startup was using, and if they weren't on AWS, we were expected to convert them, armed with relentless follow-through and a gospel of data.

The work I loved was the human part. I'd fly across the country, set up shop in the conference rooms of accelerators like Y Combinator and Techstars, and spend the day in a non stop stream of conversations. Startup after startup after startup would come in, laying bare their hopes and their problems. I mentored thousands of founders and helped hundreds migrate their infrastructure. But for every hour of human connection, there was an hour of digital penance. The CRM work was soul-crushing. After one grueling 14-hour day of back-to-back meetings, I stared at my screen and a sickening realization dawned on me: I had spent more time pasting notes into Salesforce than I had actually talking to human beings.

That's when the hacker in me, the part that instinctively rebels against a system that perverts its own mission, finally snapped. This wasn't efficiency; it was a digital assembly line designed to turn human interaction into a string of data points, and the process was so laborious it was destroying the very work it was meant to document.

So I started building tools. I created a suite of browser extensions, macros, and automation scripts that acted as a silent, invisible assistant. They filled in forms, tagged records, summarized call notes, and pre-drafted follow-up emails. They weren't complex, but they were elegant. They saved me hours —literally, four hours a night—of manual input. They gave me back the time I was supposed to be spending on my actual job: building relationships.

Months later, at a team offsite, my manager asked me to present what I'd built. I walked the team through the scripts, the simple hacks that had clawed back a third of my workday. Most were awestruck. But one colleague, who had been half listening, looked up from his laptop, his face tight with accusation.

"What the fuck, Merket?" he blurted out. "How could you hold out on us like this?"

He saw my tools not as a gift to be shared, but as a secret weapon, an unfair advantage in the fiercely competitive internal arena. His reaction was a perfect reflection of the culture: a zero-sum game where even a rising tide was suspect, because it might lift someone else's boat more than your own. We talked it through, but it was a stark lesson in how a system's incentive structures can shape the souls of the people within it. Eventually, these "Merket Hacks" became part of the official new hire onboarding—my quiet act of rebellion absorbed and sanctioned by the system itself.

But my focus began to shift from hacking the small system of my workflow to a flaw I saw in the grand strategy of the cathedral itself. It was 2015, and I could see the AI wave forming on the horizon. Startups were building incredible things on open-source frameworks like TensorFlow, and it was clear to me that the cloud provider that invested first and fastest in GPUs and AI-native tools would win the next decade. Google was already there. We were late.

At a major AWS offsite, during a Q&A with Andy Jassy, then CEO of AWS, I raised my hand. My heart pounded in the cavernous room, a drumbeat of dissent against the cathedral's silence. I asked why AWS wasn't investing more aggressively in AI startups and building the dedicated infrastructure they needed to thrive. The room went utterly still. I saw a few managers in the front rows literally roll their eyes. The question was an uncomfortable piece of grit in the gears of the machine. I stood by it. I knew the wave was coming.

What many don't know is that around that time, Sam Altman had pitched OpenAI to AWS as their first potential cloud partner. The deal fell through, from what I understood, because Amazon couldn't agree to the massive number of cloud credits OpenAI needed to train their foundational models. OpenAI went to Microsoft instead. My team had visibility into the negotiation, and for those of us who saw the future, it felt like an act of profound, world-altering frugality. We had fumbled the future.

Less than a year after my question to Jassy, AWS launched SageMaker. The cathedral was slowly turning its great mass in the right direction.

Amazon taught me discipline at a scale I could have never imagined. It taught me to lead with metrics and to think in systems. But my greatest contribution wasn't in a spreadsheet. It was in the stubborn refusal to accept that the system was always right. "Merket Hacks" was a mindset. Hacking isn't just about breaking code; it's about seeing a broken process, a flawed strategy, a missed opportunity, and refusing to let it stand. It's about building a better way, even when you're the only one who sees the need—or the only one with the nerve to say it out loud.

PART III: THE HUMAN STACK

CHAPTER 12: MIND, BODY, AND SPIRIT

There's a certain kind of pain that forces clarity—the kind that drags you, kicking and screaming, to the very edge of yourself and dares you to figure out what truly matters. For me, that pain, that brutal clarity, arrived at 4 a.m. in our Temescal neighborhood home, just two weeks after our son, Charlie, was born.

Jenn was exhausted. It was my turn to change the diaper. I went into Charlie's room, got him out of his crib, and laid him on the changing table. As I reached for the diaper cream, I fumbled and dropped it. When I bent down to pick it up, it happened. My heart, without any warning, went into a wild, terrifying, chaotic beat.

I had just gotten back from another long work trip to Bangalore, my fourteenth in two years. The night before, I'd had a single mead wine with dinner. But this wasn't about the wine. I knew what it was. Before Jenn and I had kids, we did 23andMe genetic tests. The nerd that I am, I had thoroughly researched all our potential risks. My biggest flag? Atrial fibrillation. So, when I felt my heart go into what I can only describe as a tornado-like pattern, beating at a frantic 140-180 beats per minute, I knew the diagnosis. I also knew the biggest immediate danger: throwing a stroke, because the heart isn't beating strongly enough to completely empty the left ventricle, causing blood to pool and coagulate.

My mind flashed back to the OB-GYN's office a few months earlier. Jenn was pregnant with Charlie, and we had to tell the doctor that 23andMe indicated she likely had Factor V Leiden, a genetic blood clotting disorder. "Well, how do you know this?" he asked, skeptical of the direct-to-consumer test in 2013. We explained. He was sympathetic but noted that insurance wouldn't cover the official diagnostic test unless a patient had suffered multiple miscarriages. Then he paused, looked at us, and made a decision of pure compassion. "Look," he said, "what I can do is I can change the report to say you've had three miscarriages. Then insurance will cover the official test." He did it, he ran the test, and sure enough, she was positive. We had to completely change how we managed the pregnancy. She was prescribed Lovenox, a blood thinner, to take before and after the birth to prevent a potentially fatal clot.

So, at 4 a.m., standing over my newborn son with my heart trying to beat its way out of my chest, I knew we had a supply of Lovenox disposable injectors in the fridge. My panicked, but weirdly rational, mind thought: blood clots are the danger, Lovenox is a blood thinner, this could help. The first thing I did, before anything else, was grab an injector and plunge it into my own thigh.

Jenn drove me to the ER shortly after. The diagnosis was confirmed: Afib with tachycardia. The doctors thought it best to shock my heart back into a normal rhythm. It was terrifying. You're supposed to be sedated, but I wasn't, not really. I felt and remember everything about that conversion process—the cold paddles on my chest, the jolt of electricity lifting my 6'3", 275-pound frame off the gurney, the raw, primal scream. Then, the calm words: "We got sinus." The moment was seared into me. That major pain was the start of a major shift.

After that, everything changed. I was done with the relentless travel. Those two years, largely lost to squeezing my body into coach seats inside aluminum tubes in the sky, were filled with regret. I had missed too much. I made a promise to myself, a vow: I would find a job in San Francisco that didn't require constant travel. I needed to be home. For Charlie. For Jenn. For myself.

A year later, it happened again. I was alone in an Airbnb in Kansas City after a night of indulging in BBQ and beers. I woke up around 4 a.m. with that horrifying, familiar sensation: my heart racing wildly, erratically, completely out of control. I tried the breathing tricks I'd read about. I dunked my head in ice water, trying to stimulate my vagus nerve. Nothing worked. Panic set in. Desperate, I tore through the Airbnb's kitchen and, by some miracle, found a half-empty tub of magnesium citrate powder and a lone banana. I mixed a hefty dose of the magnesium into water, choked it down, and ate the banana. I sat down at the breakfast bar, heart still hammering, bracing for another ER visit. And then, within minutes, my heart began to calm. The rhythm steadied. It returned to normal.

That moment changed everything. I became obsessed. I dove headfirst into peer-reviewed medical journals, scoured Reddit forums dedicated to Afib, and joined Facebook support groups. I learned everything I could about the intricate dance of electrolytes and their impact on heart rhythm. I started a regimen of supplements: magnesium, L-Arginine, taurine, Vitamin D. Eventually, through relentless experimentation and sheer force of will, I even taught myself how to convert out of an Afib episode using focused meditation alone. I haven't been back to the ER for my heart since.

But Afib wasn't my only physical battle around that time. I was also diagnosed with a severely herniated disc at L5-S1. The pain was unlike anything I'd ever experienced—a constant, searing agony that made sitting, standing, or even walking unbearable. I spent months essentially bedridden, lying flat on the ground, unable to work effectively, parent my newborn child, or even dress myself without wincing in pain.

I tried everything conventional medicine threw at me: chiropractors, physical therapy, multiple epidural steroid injections that offered only fleeting relief. Finally, desperate, I stumbled upon a book called Back Mechanic by Dr. Stuart McGill. I bought an inversion table. I followed his rigorous protocol religiously, decompressing my spine, re-training my core muscles, and learning new movement patterns. After months of slow, painstaking, often agonizingly painful progress—I stood up again. I walked again. I got my life back.

Healing my body taught me a profound truth that startup life, for all its lessons, hadn't: the only way out is through. You can't hustle your way past a slipped disc or a misfiring heart. You can't "growth hack" your recovery. You have to listen to your body. You have to slow down. You have to do the boring, unglamorous, often uncomfortable work of getting better, one day at a time.

But the hardest part of this journey wasn't the physical pain. It was emotional. I've carried anxiety and depression with me for most of my life—some of it likely inherited, some of it undoubtedly earned through life experiences and the accumulated wear and tear of always pushing too hard. Years of playing football and taking countless hits to the head certainly didn't help. I started therapy, reluctantly at first. I didn't want to admit I needed that kind of help; it felt like a weakness. But slowly, painstakingly, I learned how to process unresolved trauma, how to recognize the insidious spirals of negative thought patterns, how to ask for support when I needed it.

I still struggle. I take medication to ensure I can sleep through the night. I take a combination of supplements and prescribed meds just to feel functional, to feel "normal." Some days, I question if all these pills dull the edge I once prided myself on —that creative fire, the mental speed, the raw instinct. But then I look at my kids, I look at Jenn, and I remember why I do it. Because a grounded, steady version of me is what they need, what they deserve. There's no shame in needing help to function. There's no shame in building a careful scaffolding around yourself to stay upright. Stability isn't a weakness—it's a gift, especially to the people who count on you.

One night in San Francisco, after a Reddit holiday party, I was walking home when I heard a scream. A homeless man had been sleeping in front of a residential garage. The driver, apparently not seeing him in the darkness, had opened the garage door and started to pull their SUV out. The vehicle rolled over his body. I ran toward the sound. He was still alive —barely. I knelt beside him on the cold pavement, the city lights reflecting in his fading eyes. I told him to hold on, that help was coming. The fire department arrived within minutes and used a steel pole to lever the heavy vehicle off him. But it was too late. He died there, beneath that SUV, on a prosperous San Francisco street.

I think about that moment often. The sheer randomness of it. The fragility of life. How close we all are, at any given moment, to tipping over an unseen edge. That experience, more than any other, fundamentally shifted my perspective. I stopped taking things so seriously. I realized how incredibly lucky I was—how lucky we are.

That man died homeless, yet he undoubtedly had a family somewhere, people who once had dreams for him, just like my family had dreams for me. And there we were, meeting for the first and last time on such disparate sides of life's unpredictable ledger. It struck me with brutal force: one small misstep, one unlucky break, one different turn of fate, and I could have been that guy, or he could have been me. We're all just incredibly fortunate to be here, especially those of us in tech, working at world-changing companies, living comfortable lives. Yet, we're also just a hair's breadth away from not sleeping on a sidewalk in front of a garage. Life is so fucking precarious, man. That night drove home our shared humanity in a way nothing else ever had. I stopped pushing so relentlessly against the current of life and started trying to receive things as they came, to be more present with what truly mattered: my family, my friends, the simple fact of being alive and healthy. It made me stop seeing people, including myself, as systems to optimize, and start seeing pain—in others, and in myself—as something almost sacred, something to be met with compassion, not just a problem to be solved.

We glamorize resilience in the startup world. We celebrate the grind, the hustle, the ability to push through any obstacle. But real strength isn't about relentlessly pushing through everything, no matter the cost. It's about knowing when to rest. When to ask for help. When to stop pretending you're fine when you're actually falling apart.

Founders are a unique, often reckless breed. We're the ones who leap first, usually without a net. Some of us make it. Most of us don't. And a rare few get the chance to write about the journey. I'm one of the lucky ones, in more ways than I can count.

Mind, body, and spirit—if any one of them is significantly off, the others inevitably follow. I had to learn that lesson the hard, painful way. And I'm still learning, every single day. I didn't write this chapter to brag about recovery or resilience. I wrote it because someone out there needs to hear this: you can come back from the edge. You can rebuild, piece by painstaking piece. And you absolutely do not have to do it alone.

The fight for my health—my physical, mental, and spiritual well-being—wasn't a detour from my path. It was the work. It is the work. The most important startup I'll ever scale is myself. And every day I stay in that fight is a day I win.

Chapter 13: Humiliation

There are two kinds of pain. The first is a clean break. It is the shock of a car crash, the sharp verdict of a failed launch. It is loud, obvious, and commands the attention of the world. It is a story you can tell.

The second kind is a quiet corrosion. It grows in the dark, a slow tearing of the self, so private and so deeply lodged in shame that you can't give it a voice. It becomes a secret you keep not just from the world, but from yourself. You learn to build your life around it, a frantic scaffolding of performance and denial, hoping no one ever sees the rot in the foundation. For the better part of a year, I lived with both.

It began in paradise, as such things often do. October 2017. Jenn and I were in Kauai. The air was thick with salt and plumeria. But on our first night, in the rented dark, I felt a pain so sudden and so alien it felt like a violation of physics. It was as if someone had taken a recently extinguished match head and pressed it to the most vulnerable part of my body. I nearly levitated off the toilet, my vision swimming with black spots. In the bowl, there was blood. I said nothing. It was a fluke, I told myself. Dehydration. Travel. It would go away.

It did not go away. This new, private agony became the silent, humming soundtrack to a period of intense professional hope. After Amazon, my dream was to pivot to venture capital. I was rejected by a prestigious Silicon Valley firm via text message, the polite poison of the feedback—that I was "too nice" and lacked a "killer instinct"—a mortal blow delivered to the quiet of my hotel room.

Humiliation is a powerful motivator. I chose to alchemize it into fuel. Another door opened: a Kansas City seed-stage fund looking to expand to Austin. The red flags were there—the General Partner ghosting me for our first dinner meeting—but my pride was too wounded to see them clearly. I signed a risky, carry-only consulting agreement. My wife, Jenn, with her unerring intuition, hated it. But I convinced her, and myself, that it was a strategic foothold.

And so began the performance. For eleven months, I poured my soul into that firm, living a double life with excruciating precision. I sourced deals they invested in. I brought in a half-a-million-dollar check. In my one-on-ones, I was told everything was great. All the while, the secret in my body was not getting any better. The pain was no longer a visitor; it was a resident. Every bowel movement was an exercise in passing shards of glass, sending a jolt of white electricity up my spine that left me in a cold sweat, biting my own hand to keep from crying out. My life became an elaborate architecture of avoidance: standing meetings, high-top tables, a mental map of every acceptable bathroom in Austin.

After ten months, a GI doctor finally gave the corrosion a name: an anal fissure. A tear in a place that can never truly rest. He prescribed creams. They didn't work. At my follow-up, he laid out the final option: surgery. They would have to cut the internal sphincter muscle itself. Then came the caveat, delivered with sterile detachment. There was a non-zero, statistically significant chance that cutting the muscle would cause permanent fecal incontinence.

There it was. The word hung in the air of that small, beige room. Incontinence. A verdict on my dignity, my manhood, my future. My choice: live with this invisible, daily agony, or risk shitting my pants for the rest of my life.

That was the decision I was wrestling with as I painfully drove to Houston for a big meeting I had sourced for the firm. The night before, the partner called me down to the hotel lobby for a "debrief."

The lobby was cavernous, the ceiling hundreds of feet tall. The air hummed with the anonymous chatter of business travelers. I saw them sitting at a small table and walked over, my palms already slick with a familiar, anxious sweat. My stomach was a queasy knot. I was sure this was a reprimand. Maybe the LP search for their second fund wasn't going well enough. Maybe I needed to focus more on deal flow.

I made some awkward small talk. "How did you sleep last night?"

The GP gave a non-committal answer. He looked anxious, too. Scared. He was not in a good place. He took a breath, and the performance began.

"Ryan," he started, his voice low, "this is going to be one of the hardest things I've ever had to do."

The ambient noise of the lobby—the clinking glasses, the low murmur of conversation—faded into a dull roar.

"Unfortunately, we are going to have to go a different direction." I was stunned.

"What? You just told me two weeks ago in my one-on-one that everything was great."

"Yeah, I realize that," he said, his eyes fixed on a point somewhere over my shoulder, a classic tell of a man trying to distance himself from his own words. "Maybe I shouldn't have played a passive management style..."

The words were armor for him, meaningless corporate speak designed to absolve him of the moment. He kept talking, but I barely heard it. I felt a surge of emotion at the table, a hot flush of shame and anger, but I held it in. Eleven months of work. No paycheck. Evaporated. Betrayed.

I don't remember what I said. I just remember standing up, turning, and walking out, my suitcase dragging behind me like an anchor. The air outside was damp and cool; it had been raining. I got into my truck, the silence of the cab a shocking contrast to the noise in my head.

I started driving, pulling onto the feeder road, my hands trembling on the wheel. I didn't want to cry in front of him. I didn't want to give him that. But as I merged, as the truck accelerated and the highway lights began to streak past, the dam finally broke.

I don't remember the drive home from Houston. It's a black hole in my memory. What I remember is pulling over on the side of I-10, somewhere east of San Antonio where the landscape is flat and unforgiving. I couldn't sit anymore. The pain from my body and the pain from my life had converged into a single, unbearable pressure. The scaffolding had finally collapsed. I got out of my truck and stood on the shoulder, the indifferent Texas sun beating down, the scream of 18-wheelers roaring past like mechanical beasts. I was a static object of failure in a world that was moving too fast. My body was broken. My spirit was broken. My dream was a heap of smoking wreckage. I was nothing.

I pulled out my phone and called my friend Micah Baldwin. He picked up immediately. I stood there on the side of the road, the asphalt shimmering with heat, and I sobbed. Not quiet tears, but the ugly, ragged, heaving sobs of a man who had nothing left. I told him everything. The pain. The surgery choice. The firing. The humiliation. He didn't offer solutions or platitudes. He just listened. He held the space. He let me be broken.

When I got home later that night, I pulled out my contract. I read the bullet points. The first one wasn't about raising money for some future fund. It was about bringing in quality deals. It was exactly what I had been doing.

A few weeks later, I had the surgery. The recovery was a new circle of hell, a level of pain that made the previous year feel like a prelude. For a time, the fear of incontinence was a daily, terrifying reality. It was a dark, dark time. It took a full year for my body to feel like it belonged to me again. There is no neat lesson here.

There is no triumphant comeback at the end of this chapter. There is only the grim reality of the bottom, the place where you are betrayed by others and by your own body, all at once. The world doesn't stop for your suffering. But if you are lucky, one person will answer the phone. And if you are lucky, after some time in the dark, you find the will to take a single, agonizing step forward.

It wasn't a comeback. It was an act of survival. And for a long, long time, it was all I had.

CHAPTER 14: GOODFAIR AND THE UNBOXING REVOLUTION

In early 2019, a few months after being let go from the VC firm, I jumped aboard a Houston-based startup called Goodfair. The mission was simple but incredibly powerful: reduce the colossal problem of textile waste by selling curated, thrifted mystery clothing bundles online. Think subscription box meets sustainability, with a dash of treasure hunt thrown in. It was quirky, scrappy, undeniably purpose-driven, and tackling a real-world problem—precisely the kind of challenge I live for.

We had some early traction on Instagram, but my gut told me something bigger was brewing over on TikTok. Gen Z was migrating there in droves, and the platform's "For You" algorithm was a veritable virality factory. I quietly made a small tweak to our website's "Thank You" page after a purchase, adding a single line of text: "We love seeing your unboxing videos on TikTok! Use #goodfair and we'll promote the best ones." No splashy campaign, no ad spend. Just a simple, open invitation to create and share.

Three weeks later, on Easter Sunday 2020, I opened our sales dashboard and nearly dropped my phone. Orders were flooding in, literally by the second. Our website traffic had exploded. A quick search on

TikTok revealed the cause: two Goodfair unboxing videos had gone massively viral. We went from our average daily sales figures to a staggering 26X spike, almost overnight. The raw power of authentic, user-generated content on a platform built for discovery was awe-inspiring.

By Monday morning, we were virtually shaking hands with Imaginary Ventures—the esteemed NYC-based venture capital firm behind breakout brands like Glossier and Skims. They had been circling us for a potential Seed round, and this explosive, organic growth was precisely the proof they needed. In a single, whirlwind weekend, our customers had effectively funded our investment round for us.

We were riding an incredible high. We were hiring rapidly, expanding operations, and felt like we were genuinely doing something real and impactful. The flywheel was spinning at an almost dizzying pace: enthusiastic Gen Z influencers, the magic of TikTok virality, and a compelling sustainable mission all locking into place perfectly.

But as any seasoned entrepreneur knows, beneath the gleaming surface of rapid growth, cracks can begin to appear. And in the brutal, unforgiving world of e-commerce, those cracks can quickly become chasms. Fulfillment is a beast Logistics are a daily firefight. Inventory management for one-of-a-kind thrifted items was a unique kind of chaos. We were operating in the COVID era, a time of cash, cash everywhere.

People were receiving stimulus checks from the government and spending that money online like it was going out of style. And because of those viral TikTok user generated videos, we were getting SLAMMED with orders. Just utterly slammed. We couldn't keep up.

The hacker's ethos isn't about breaking things; it's about finding the single leverage point that hanges the entire game. It's the relentless hunt for the one byte of code, or the one business decision, that unlocks everything.

Our warehouse operations, strained beyond capacity, started to buckle. We began shipping the wrong SKUs in the wrong boxes. Our quality control processes, vital for a business dealing in pre-owned goods, broke down. In one particularly disastrous and publicly embarrassing incident, we let political shirts slip through the cracks. An LGBTQ+ Black Lives Matter supporter live-streamed their Goodfair mystery box unboxing, only to pull out a Webb County Sheriff appreciation shirt. Yeah, not good. The negative viral video spread like wildfire, a painful counterpoint to our earlier successes.

Because of these escalating product quality and fulfillment issues, our Return on Ad Spend (ROAS) on

Facebook and other platforms started to suffer. Yet, we felt compelled to keep spending, chasing the venture capital-fueled growth targets we thought we needed to reach the next funding round.

Seeing the inherent unpredictability and the escalating QC challenges of the mystery box model, my old hacker mindset kicked into high gear. To me, this wasn't just a business problem; it was a complex system with a critical bug that was causing a negative user experience.

So I started to do what I've always done: I *reverse-engineered the problem*. I was looking for the single leverage point, that one thing I could change that would alter the entire outcome.

It was just like my early days cracking software—if you could find that one function handling the copy protection and change just the right bytes of code, you could unlock everything.

Here, the "bug" wasn't a line of code; it was the mystery itself. The "patch," therefore, had to be a reduction of that mystery.

I began advocating fiercely for a strategic pivot. I proposed that we invest in our own line of "branded pre-owned" shirts. The concept was simple: we'd buy bales of high-quality, used, blank t-shirts from clothing recyclers—garments that would otherwise be shipped overseas and likely end up in landfills.

We'd then partner with a local printer to emblazon them with the Goodfair logo and our sustainability message. We could sell these for around 90% margins, offering customers a product they knew they wanted while still fulfilling our core mission.

The branded strategy started showing immediate promise. It was so promising, in fact, that we were invited to be a t-shirt vendor at a major music festival, where the plan was to sell festival-branded shirts printed on our used Goodfair blanks. It required a significant upfront investment, but I truly felt it was the right direction for the company. It was the elegant hack the system needed.

Despite A-list celebs and streamers popping up with Goodfair branded sweatshirts, the leadership team couldn't achieve alignment on this new direction. Ultimately, the decision was made to forgo the "branded" strategy and double down on the original, struggling mystery thrift product. It was around that time, seeing the writing on the wall and recognizing the need to conserve cash, that I decided it would be best for me to step down to save the company runway.

Goodfair never did raise that next round. Eventually, the company was bought out of bankruptcy by one of its clothing recycler vendors. I believe it's still operating in some form today. Godspeed to them.

Looking back, Goodfair wasn't a failure in my eyes. Not really. We proved a new kind of e-commerce playbook could work. We pioneered the unboxing model in the circular economy. We made thousands of young people genuinely excited to buy and wear secondhand clothes. But I left with the undeniable pang of knowing we hadn't finished what we started. Startups can break your heart that way. You see something special, you feel it working, you pour your soul into it—and then the market, or internal dynamics, or just plain bad luck, reminds you that feeling isn't always enough.

One key lesson from that whirlwind: going out of stock is okay. Sometimes it's even a good sign. As a startup, you have to be constantly launching new products, testing the market, and learning. You can't be afraid to pivot, to diversify your revenue streams, and to manage risk proactively.

I'm still incredibly proud of what we built at Goodfair. I'm proud of that one little line of text that ignited a firestorm of creativity. I'm proud of the dedicated team who tirelessly picked and packed orders in those Houston warehouses when things got unimaginably wild. And I'm proud that for a brief, shining moment, we made the internet care deeply about secondhand clothes.

Goodfair didn't scale into the unicorn we all hoped for. But it mattered. And sometimes, that's enough.

CHAPTER 15: PUBLIC FAILURE

After years of working inside big companies and helping other founders scale their ventures, the itch returned. It always does. This time, I saw a massive wave forming in the crypto space, specifically with NFTs. I believed they were poised to become a vital part of a marketer's toolkit for building community and engaging with customers. I still do. But as any founder knows, vision is one thing; timing is everything.

With that belief, I started Mission Labs. It breaks my heart to say it, but the venture is now officially wound down. It was my biggest professional failure to date, a painful, humbling, and incredibly clarifying experience.

For the sake of full transparency, and to honor the lessons learned, the best way to tell this story is to share the email I sent to our pre-seed investors and eventually posted to my personal blog:

Hello all,

This email is one of the hardest I've ever had to write.

Unfortunately, after much deliberation and last-minute deals falling through, I have started the wind-down process for Mission Labs, Inc.

What I did wrong:

1) Hired too fast: I hired a team before hitting product-market fit, convinced the NFT boom would be more prolonged and pronounced than it was. This caused us to get bogged down in corporate-like meetings when we needed a singular focus on product and customer conversations. I expected our seed round was just around the corner, back when capital was much cheaper in the Spring. I was wrong.

2) Hired wrong: Most of the initial team did not have Web3 experience. I thought we could overcome this with training, but the learning curve proved too steep, bogging the company down with elementary questions and confusion.

3) Selected a name & branding that attracted legal action: We took too long to settle on a name: Momintous. I didn't do a thorough-enough trademark search. Four months after a LinkedIn post announced our new branding, Momentive.ai (the parent company of SurveyMonkey) sent us a cease & desist letter due to our names being too similar in their opion. As a small, pre-seed company, this seriously derailed us, wasting precious time and capital.

4) Services work: I thought we could offset our initial R&D costs by doing one-off NFT drops for artists and brands. This was a huge distraction. It took all hands on deck just to get the one store we did live, and the artist's adult-themed work made it difficult to use as a case study for the mainstream brands we were targeting.

5) Delegated finances: I delegated finances to my co-founder, who is not a CPA. We lost one to two months of runway simply due to not having an accurate read on our burn rate.

6) Delegated Update e-mail: At my first startup, I wrote weekly investor updates religiously. This time, my team wanted to own it, but only do it monthly. I relented. We missed a few months in a row. I eventually took it back over. Next time, it's weekly, and I'm writing them.

7) NFTs fell out of favor with Gen Z: The environmental impact of Proof-of-Work blockchains gave NFTs a negative connotation. When Gen Z turned against them, the brands targeting that market vanished overnight. I noticed this trend early but waited too long to pivot away from the term *"NFTs"* and toward the intrinsic value they brought to collectors and artists.

8) Employees vs. Contractors: In hindsight, except for my cofounders, I should have started everyone as contractors. The cost of employees is high, and it's hard to know who will make it in the early days.

9) More angels, fewer funds: When I started, every VC fund in Texas was reaching out. Flattered, I met with them all. It was a waste of time. I wasn't ready for those meetings and probably killed any shot of raising from them for this venture. First impressions are huge. I should have kept my head down, said "thanks but no thanks" to the meeting invites, and focused on building the product and raising from angels and strategic investors first.

What's Next?

I explored launching a new blockchain with the Mission Labs assets, but ultimately my heart wasn't in it. I will take some time off to rest (my wife's orders) and then get back at it. I will most likely take a job as we head into a time of uncertainty, so I can recalibrate. But I am always looking for the next venture. Thank you to all of you for believing in me. Seriously, it crushes me to know I won't be returning your money on this company. I will always be eternally grateful for your support and trust in me. When I launch my next company, you will be the first to know.

I am working with my legal team to wind down the company... Thank you from the bottom of my heart.

Ryan Merket

Sharing that failure so publicly is terrifying. But the hacker's mindset isn't just about finding clever solutions; it's about rigorously reverse-engineering your own mistakes. It's about staring at the wreckage, figuring out exactly which lines of code—or which decisions—caused the crash, and learning from it so the next build is stronger.

This was my crash. And these are my lessons.

CHAPTER 16: BROTHERHOOD AND THE LONG ROAD TRIP

Of all the partnerships and teams I've built, one of the most important has been with Nicholas Laning, the man I call my brother. We were born just two days apart in the same hospital.

Our mothers were best friends in high school and later college roommates at Texas Tech. Growing up, even though we almost always lived in different cities, our families made sure we were inseparable. They would fly us back and forth between California and Texas, organize family vacations to meet up, and even send VHS tapes through the mail—personal video messages of their family adventures, addressed just to us.

"Hey Merket's, we miss you guys, we are at Big Bend National Park!" It was a bond forged before we could even form memories.

Years later, after his first marriage ended, Nick was in a really low spot. I knew things weren't going well, but my own life was a blur of constant travel. I was on a plane all the time, in another country, and I couldn't be there for him as much as I wanted to, as much as he needed me to be. It's a regret I still carry. After I sold Appbistro to InMobi and finally had a stretch of time without travel, Nick gave me a call. The divorce was finalized. He said, "I need you."

So I flew to Dallas, and we took a road trip to the 5F Ranch, a remote spot three hours away, outside Zephyr, Texas. We talked. We laughed. We cried. We let the vast, quiet landscape of Texas fill our souls and begin to heal the parts of him that were broken. His photography business was struggling, and he needed help getting to where he knew he could be: one of Texas's top wedding photographers. He had the talent, but at that moment, what he really needed was confidence. The confidence to go out and land the big deals that would change his career.

That's when it hit me. I was just starting my new job at Amazon, a role that would require more travel. What if I brought him with me? He could set up local photo shoots in different cities beforehand. I had a ton of saved-up airline miles, and I could just get hotel rooms with two beds.

So that's what we did.

Our first trip was to Seattle. It was a boring trip for me, just some standard Amazon training. But for Nick? It was a creative explosion. He walked for miles, shooting the city, and even booked a few engagement sessions. With his confidence starting to build, so did my travel schedule.

We hit New York City, Tokyo, Mexico City. With each trip, Nick got more and more work. His portfolio grew, and so did his reputation.

He quickly remarried, finding the best life and business partner he could ask for, and they now have a beautiful little daughter. Today, they are, without question, among Texas's top wedding and fashion photographers, with numerous accolades and articles celebrating their stunning work.

We still take those work trips together when we can. It's our way of connecting, a necessary tradition in the midst of the wonderful busyness of our lives and families. It's a reminder that sometimes the best way to "hack" a problem isn't with code or a clever business strategy, but with loyalty, with showing up, with offering a friend a plane ticket and a second bed in a hotel room, and giving them the space to rediscover their own edge.

CHAPTER 17: SHOWING UP

If there's a single, non-negotiable line of code in my personal operating system, it's loyalty. It's a deep, foundational part of who I am, a value that has guided me—and, admittedly, gotten me into trouble—for my entire life. It's the instinct that made me want to get into a fistfight over my friend Matt Trussell's keyed truck back in high school. The expression of that loyalty has matured since then, evolving from teenage brawling to something quieter but, I hope, more impactful. It's about showing up.

I have friends like Bradley Myers and Nicholas Laning who have been in my life since childhood; I still talk to them almost every day. That kind of long-term trust is something I cherish. It's a bond that, once forged, I feel compelled to honor, especially when life gets hard. For me, that often manifests in trying to be the friend who can provide help, not just sympathy.

A few years ago, a friend I've known for a very long time got out of jail. He was starting over with nothing—no car, no job, no clear path forward. He needed a fresh start, but it's nearly impossible to get back on your feet when you can't even get to a job interview. So, I went on Carvana, bought him a car, and had it delivered. It was a practical solution to an immediate problem. That single act of support has since had a ripple effect—he got a whole new grill, his confidence is back, and he's had a crazy, positive transformation. I'm incredibly proud of him.

More recently, another friend from middle school was facing an agonizing situation. Their child identifies as LGBTQ+, and given the political climate and new laws in Texas, they no longer felt safe here. They needed to move to a state where their child could grow up without fear, but they didn't have the money to just pick up and restart their lives. So I asked them to calculate exactly what it would take—the moving truck, the first month's rent, the security deposit, everything. The number was close to $18,000. I started sending them weekly payments of a few thousand dollars until they had what they needed to make the move. They did it. They're safe now.

I don't share these stories to pat myself on the back, but to explain how I view the bonds of friendship. When someone has earned my trust, I feel a duty to be there, to offer what I can—whether it's a car, rent money, or just flying out for a weekend to help them through a divorce. But that loyalty, as deep as it runs, is not unconditional. It's a two-way street built on trust, and it can be broken. People have done it. The founding team of Ping.fm is a perfect example. After that betrayal, my loyalty to them was gone. It has to be. My rule is simple:

if you treat me right, I will always treat you right, and I will never forget the kindness and trust you showed me.

Ultimately, for me, this all comes back to my faith. I believe this is what God would want us to do—to be our brother's keeper, to lift up our friends when they fall, to use whatever resources we have to serve the people we love. It's not just about being a good friend; it's what makes me feel happy, what makes me feel human. It's the quiet, steady work of showing up, an unwritten contract of loyalty that, for me, is the most meaningful bottom line there is.

CHAPTER 18: THE AUSTIN BUILD

"I made a promise to myself that I would always be there for both of you boys in any activities you were involved in." - Jim Merket

The decision to leave the constant travel behind and join Reddit was a direct result of my health crisis and a vow to be a more present father and husband. But the reality of those early years of parenthood, even without the international flights, was its own intense crucible.

Charlie was a very challenging baby. As an infant, he was borderline colic, wracked by crying spells we couldn't seem to soothe. I remember one particularly desperate night when we ended up in the children's ER in Oakland because he simply would not stop crying. He was just done, exhausted by his own distress. The diagnosis was simple—gas—but the experience was harrowing. It felt horrible to think about how much I had been traveling during his first two years, leaving Jenn to manage so much of this on her own. We didn't have any

parents or family nearby to help. It was just her, fielding my calls from different time zones while trying to calm a distraught baby. She would text and call, her voice frayed with emotional exhaustion. It was hard. It put an immense strain on us as a couple and as new parents. But around the six-month mark, things started to shift. We slowly found a routine that seemed to work, finding our footing together.

And amidst the challenges, there were moments of pure magic that gave us glimpses into the unique person Charlie was becoming. We started to notice his incredible memory. He was obsessed with Thomas the Train, and he could memorize every single character by face alone. Jenn would cover up an entire train toy except for its tiny, painted face, and without fail, Charlie would be able to decipher exactly who it was. It was astounding, a little spark of the amazing mind he was developing.

Those sparks, those challenges, and the daily grind of parenting in the demanding Bay Area environment led to another pivotal realization. When we got pregnant with our second child, Stella, in 2016, we knew something had to change fundamentally. If we were going to have more children, we couldn't do it alone on an island far from our roots. We needed to be closer to family.

So, we started to look for houses in Austin, Texas. My parents were in nearby New Braunfels, and my brother's family was in Kyle. Moving to the Austin area just made sense. It was a deliberate choice to prioritize family infrastructure and support over proximity to the Silicon Valley epicenter. We eventually found a home and settled into the Circle C neighborhood in South Austin.

The change was immediate and profound. Being so close to family has been huge. We see them for every birthday, every holiday, and most of our kids' sporting events. The constant, low-level stress of being without a support system vanished, replaced by the easy comfort of having grandparents, aunts, uncles, and cousins just a short drive away. It's been great. Professionally, the move didn't mean unplugging from the world I loved; it meant re-grounding it. When we first moved,

I was still working for Amazon, and my role on the AWS Startup Team allowed me to quickly get involved with the burgeoning local startup scene in Austin. I started mentoring founders at local accelerators and incubators, building a new network while leveraging my old one. I still make it back to San Francisco pretty regularly for demo days, board meetings, and conferences, so I don't feel like I'm out of the ecosystem. I've just changed my home base.

I'm still making regular angel investments, still hunting for those passionate, underdog founders with a unique edge. But now, the process looks a little different. It's calmer, more integrated into the life we've built here. The other day, I wasreviewing a pitch deck on my laptop, and Charlie came over, peered at the screen with intense curiosity, and started asking questions. My two worlds—the "hacker" and the "father"— had finally, beautifully, merged.

I'm still mentoring. I'm still investing. But now, I have Charlie and Stella to help me look over the deals.

CHAPTER 19: LEGACY CODE

For most of my life, I've tried to understand my own operating system. I've traced the origins of my anxiety, my deep-seated need for loyalty, and the relentless, sometimes self-destructive, drive that has propelled me. I looked for the source in my own experiences—in the schoolyard, in the glow of a CRT monitor, in the wreckage of a failed startup.

The answers, I'm finding, weren't in my own code base. They were in my father's.

In a collection of stories he wrote late in his life, my dad, Jim, laid his own code bare. And in his words, I found the ghost in my machine. He wrote about his own father, a man who came back from World War II with a trauma he couldn't name and tried to drown in alcohol. My dad wrote:

"He would drink and was not a very nice drunk as he would get angry and break furniture, which scared the hell out of an eight-year old and I would hide under my bed and cover my ears with my pillow. I do not wonder where my anxiety disorder originated from."

Reading that line was like finding a hidden comment in my own source code, explaining a function I never understood.

Neither do I, Dad.

He wrote about feeling safe only when his father wasn't home. He wrote about a man who never really said "I love you," who showed affection through the awkward gift of a $100 bill or by buying a swing set for the grandkids he rarely saw. A man who, in a moment of shocking loyalty, defended my parents against a harassing cop, but who mostly remained a figure of intimidation and fear.

But then I found the patch. It was the piece of code my father wrote to fix the bug for the next generation. It was the most important line in his entire story, and it has become the most important line in mine. After describing the pain and neglect from his own dad, he wrote:

"Therefore, I made a promise to myself that I would always be there for both of you boys in any activities you were involved in."

There it was. The vow. The source code for every time he showed up to one of our games. The reason he took pride in our accomplishments. He was actively, consciously trying to be the father he never had.

And I see now that my own life has been an unconscious echo of that vow. My fierce, sometimes foolish, loyalty to my friends; the guilt that tore me apart when I was traveling constantly, missing my own son's infancy; the ultimate decision to trade global ambition for a quiet life in Austin where I can coach my kids' teams—it's all there. I have been trying to live up to my father's promise, and perhaps, trying to perfect it for the generation that follows me. The anxiety may be the ghost

I inherited, but the loyalty—the drive to show up —is the legacy I choose to claim.

PART IV: THE EDGE

CHAPTER 20: AN EXISTENTIAL THREAT

If I've spent this book talking about hacking systems, it's because I believe systems—whether they're made of code, or business plans, or social norms—are meant to be understood, questioned, and improved. But for the last several years, I've been watching the most important system I know—American democracy—being hacked by forces I believe pose an existential threat to our future. Leaving this part of my story out would be a lie of omission. My political convictions aren't separate from who I am; they are a fundamental part of my operating system.

I've always been a staunch believer in progressive policies. I was a huge Bernie Sanders supporter, and I was, frankly, traumatized by the way the Democratic establishment seemed to systematically dismantle his campaign during his primary run against Hillary Clinton. It felt like a betrayal of the grassroots energy he was building. That experience left me deeply cynical about the political machinery, and it also gave me a clear-eyed view of the 2016 general election.

I never voted for Trump, but I was convinced he was going to beat HRC. The context of the situation was just too potent. Clinton was heavily disliked by independents and the right; Russia was hacking her campaign manager's emails and weaponizing them through Wikileaks, allowing them to command the media airwaves; and the raw, populist energy Trump was attracting was undeniable. It just felt like he was going to win. So, I did what a hacker with a brokerage account does: I placed a large options trade, betting that the stock market would crash in the immediate aftermath of a Trump victory.

Then came the night of November 8th, 2016. I will never, ever forget it. It was a surreal split-screen of personal miracle and national crisis. As the election results poured in, confirming my grim prediction, Jenn went into labor. In the early morning hours, our daughter, Stella, was born. As baby and momma slept, I stared at my phone, watching the world react to the dawn of the first Trump presidency. And just as I predicted, the futures market was in freefall. It was crashing. I was right. In that bizarre, sleep-deprived moment, I felt a dizzying mix of emotions: the profound joy of holding my new daughter, and the bittersweet, vindicating thrill of having made a bunch of money by correctly calling the election. I finally went to sleep feeling as good as one possibly can when their country has just lurched into a dark, uncertain future.

I woke up the next morning to the beautiful, immediate crisis of baby Stella learning how to take a nipple. I said good morning to my loves, my heart full, and picked up my phone to check my profits.

Oh, no.

Overnight, the markets had completely reversed. To my dismay, Wall Street had decided that a Trump presidency, with its promises of deregulation and tax cuts, would actually be great for business. The market rallied with astonishing speed. My options were now worthless. I had lost the whole trade. Ugh. A new daughter, a new president, and a financial gut punch, all in less than 12 hours.

That shock propelled me into action. When Beto O'Rourke launched his Senate campaign against Ted Cruz in Texas, I went all in. This felt like the first real battle against the tide. I used my expertise to help his campaign's ad agency run targeted ads on Reddit, trying to leverage the platform for political change. When he lost, despite the massive grassroots energy and a nationwide sense of hope, that's when I knew things were truly, deeply fucked. Even after seeing what Trump was doing, Texas still voted for Ted Cruz. The propaganda was working. Fox News, Newsmax, and a universe of social media influencers were working in tandem to, in my view, brainwash people—including some of my own friends and family. It's a profound sadness that I still carry. It makes me weep for this country and for the future my children will inherit.

The hacker in me needs to understand the "why." How does this happen? I believe a huge part of the answer lies in a statistic that should terrify every American: over half of our adult population (54%) reads below a sixth-grade level, and nearly one in five reads below a third-grade level. When a population struggles with basic literacy, complex policy debates become irrelevant. It becomes less about what a candidate will do and more about how they make you feel. Trump and his campaign manager, Steve Bannon, understood this intuitively. They realized that emotion, grievance, and identity were the most powerful leverage points in the system. From the moment Trump stepped off that golden elevator in Trump Tower to announce his presidency in 2015, he played the biggest, most potent emotional card he had: racism. He famously went off-script to say, "When Mexico sends its people, they're not sending their best... They're bringing drugs, they're bringing crime, they're rapists. And some, I assume, are good people."

That was the opening salvo. From then until now, the "us vs. them" mentality has been the central operating principle, a strategy that catapulted him into the White House and has kept him at the forefront of American politics ever since. It's a hack of our oldest and ugliest divisions, amplified by modern media, and it's working with devastating effectiveness. And for me, this isn't a political game. It's an existential threat to the pluralistic, democratic system I believe in, and the fight against it has become an undeniable part of my story.

CHAPTER 21: THE RIVER

When my parents moved us back from California to Texas the summer before my sixth grade, we landed in New Braunfels. It's a small, German-Texas town south of Austin, defined by two things: its history and its rivers. My parents moved my brother and me into a small, shotgun-style house on Albert Street, right across from the Guadalupe River. That house, and the water flowing just a stone's throw from our front door, became the center of my universe.

The Guadalupe was wild, a Texan version of Pleasure Island from Pinocchio. The Comal, its spring-fed counterpart, was our personal playground. Between them was Schlitterbahn, the massive waterpark where we spent our summers. New Braunfels was, in every sense, a kid's dream, a piece of my childhood I'm so grateful my own kids now get to experience.

But the town offered more than just an escape; it offered a spark. In 7th grade, I signed up for theater with the legendary Mr. Watson. He was amazing, providing the discipline I secretly craved. On the first day of class, he told us about his other passion: New York City. Every summer, he took a group of 7th and 8th graders there to see the sights and a couple of Broadway plays. All you needed was $1,200 plus spending money.

I was floored. The idea of New York was as foreign and magical as the surface of the moon. I raced home and told my Mom, my words tumbling out in a torrent of excitement. Her response was kind but firm, a gentle closing of a door I hadn't even realized I was standing in front of. "Yeah... we are not paying for that."

It wasn't just disappointment I felt. It was a challenge. In my world, a "no" like that wasn't a closed door. It was a lock to be picked, a system to be figured out. A mentality I've had all mylife. When someone tells me I can't or shouldn't do something, I find a way to prove them wrong. The dream wasn't dead; the hunt had just begun.

A couple of months later, on a cool fall day in late September, I was back in the Guadalupe. The summer crowds were gone, but the water was still swimmable. I was out with my friend Nick Laning (who I mentioned earlier), not looking for a miracle, just having fun, hoping to find a lost pair of Oakleys or a pocket knife. We had a tactic for the rapids: one of us would act as a human dam, blocking the current, while the other would use goggles to hunt on the shallow riverbed. We agreed to split whatever we found, fiftyfifty.

Nick was blocking the water, and I was searching right below a large rock, my face submerged in the cool, clear current. I was scanning the familiar landscape of river stones when a glimmer caught my eye. It was different from the muted shine of wet quartz. This was a sharp, brilliant flash. Normal rocks don't glimmer like that.

My heart started to race. I was running out of breath, but I reached down, about four feet, and my fingers closed around something small and hard. I knew as soon as I grabbed it that it was a ring. I brought it up to my goggles. I could see the diamond. The question hit me with a jolt: "Is it costume? Is it fake?" I made an inaudible grunt, my lungs burning. I had to go up for air. I broke the surface, took a huge gasp, and went back down. It was still there. My heart was going nuts as I grabbed it for good and shot back to the surface.

I had never found a diamond ring before. I'd found silver rings, charms, sunglasses, but this was different from the moment I saw it. I broke the surface, holding it up to the Texas sun.

"I found a ring!" I yelled to Nick. "Let's go!"

We were ecstatic, running back to my house, the biggest treasure I had ever found clutched in my hand. We later found out it was 1.3 karats. It was a big diamond. My mom, ever the pragmatist, said we could only keep it if no one claimed it after we ran an ad in the local newspaper's lost and found for 30 days.

Those were the longest 30 days of my life. The process took months to play out, a slow burn of anticipation. Finally, with no one claiming it, she took the ring to a jeweler at USAA. They bought it on the spot for $1,400.

The money was my ticket. My mom used it to pay for my trip to New York. In the dizzying excitement of it all, I conveniently forgot about Nick's half. It was a selfish, teenage oversight, a promise that got lost in the shuffle of my own ambition. Nick didn't mention it until years later, and when he did, I felt an insane, retroactive pang of guilt. It's a debt I hope I've since repaid through the years of friendship and the ways I've tried to show up for him, a quiet reminder of the complexities that get tangled up even in our purest moments of joy.

That trip, funded by the river, changed my life. Standing on top of the Empire State Building, seeing the Statue of Liberty up close, getting lost in the beautiful, overwhelming chaos of Chinatown, watching The Phantom of the Opera from a velvet seat—it shattered the confines of my small-town world. It wasn't just seeing the sights; it was the reprogramming of my own expectations. It planted a single, powerful question in my mind that has guided me ever since:

"Why not me?"

When I got home, I wallpapered my entire bedroom with a massive mural of the New York City skyline, complete with the Twin Towers. I stared at that skyline every day for years, a constant reminder of the feeling of possibility. I never lost that confidence. The next time I was back in New York City, I wasn't a wide-eyed 7th grader. I was on stage in front of thousands, launching my first real startup at TechCrunch Disrupt.

Today, my venture fund is called Comal Ventures. I named it after the river that gave me more than just a place to swim. It gave me a treasure that funded a dream, which in turn gave me the audacity to believe I could build a life beyond its banks. The river is where my edge was forged.

CHAPTER 22: THE OTHER SIDE OF THE TABLE

A real startup idea isn't a business plan. It's a virus. It infects a founder's mind, hijacking their every waking thought, rewriting their priorities, and compelling them to abandon the safety of a normal life. It's a beautiful, terrifying, all-consuming sickness. I know, because I've had the disease. I've got the scar tissue to prove it.

And that scar tissue is the single greatest difference between a founder and the vast majority of venture capitalists. It's why I have a deep, almost cellular empathy for anyone crazy enough to be in the early stages of a build. When I sit across the table from a founder, I don't see a line on a spreadsheet or a potential 10x return. I see the sleepless nights. I see the relationship strain. I see the quiet, gut-wrenching terror of watching the bank account dwindle. I see a fellow veteran of a war that most people, especially those who control the capital, have only ever read about.

Most VCs are just tourists in the land of creation, and they treat founders like the local help. They've never had to make payroll with their own savings. They've never been betrayed by a co-founder. They've never had to stare at the ceiling at 3 a.m., crushed by the weight of their employees' mortgages. They quote episodes of Billions because they think it's a playbook, not realizing it's a satire about the very soulless, money-obsessed culture they perpetuate. They don't give a shit about founders; they give a shit about their fund's IRR (returns to THEIR investors). They are money managers, not builders.

And let's be clear: leading a new team inside a billion-dollar company is not a "startup." It's intrapreneurship. It's a valuable skill, but it's not the same game. You have a safety net the size of a continent. You aren't risking your own ruin. You haven't stared into the abyss. Don't ever confuse the two. I decided early on that if I was ever in a position to write a check, I would be the investor I wished I'd had. I wanted to be like the guys who helped me when I had nothing to offer in return—people like Paul Bragiel and Steve Jang, who would take a meeting at a coffee shop and open up their networks without a second thought. They were paying it forward, operating on a code of shared experience.

After the Facebook IPO and the InMobi acquisition, I finally had the capital to do more than just offer advice. I started writing small angel checks. Most, as expected, went to zero. But then, a few started to connect. I backed smart, direct-toconsumer plays like Apostrophe, a teledermatology company that was later acquired by Hims & Hers. I invested in deep tech, like Freshplum, which was acquired by Twitter after TellApart (another of my investments) was acquired by them, and Threatcare, a cybersecurity startup founded by the brilliant Marcus Carey that was acquired by ReliaQuest. I was betting on builders who saw a clear problem and had the grit to solve it.

But the one that got me truly hooked was one of my earliest investments: Ankur Nagpal's company, Teachable. I saw that virus in him—that relentless, obsessive drive. I wrote a check. The company went on to be acquired in a deal that returned 25 times my investment. The financial return was incredible, but the real prize was the confirmation of the model: I got to meet and help amazing founders—people with the same disease as me—and I could get paid for it? It felt like I had hacked the system, finding a way to stay in the game on my own terms.

Since then, I have made over 200 angel investments. I've backed audacious, world-changing ideas like Colossal Biosciences' work on de-extinction. I've backed founders I knew and respected, like my former boss at Reddit, Yishan Wong, and his massively ambitious mission at Terraformation to reverse climate change by reforesting the planet. I've made personal bets on companies I believed in deeply, like purchasing early stock options in Reddit.

For years, helping founders was my personal passion project. But as my work in Austin deepened, I knew it was time to give it a name, a home, a flag to fly. That's when I founded Comal Ventures, a brand for my personal investing and founder mentoring, named after the river that gave me my first taste of a life-changing return. It's my way of honoring my roots while betting on the future.

It's still just me, writing checks, taking late-night calls, and trying to be the investor who remembers what the scar tissue feels like. But who knows? Maybe raising a formal fund—a cathedral of capital built on a foundation of empathy, with a sign on the door that says

"Builders Only"—is the next chapter. Maybe it's time to hack the system at scale.

CONCLUSION: THE EDGE IS YOURS

So, there you have it. My story, or at least a significant slice of it – from a kid cracking code in a Texas bedroom to navigating the dizzying highs and gut-wrenching lows of the tech world, and somehow finding my way through addiction, imposter syndrome, and the constant, beautiful chaos of life. Laying it all out like this, chapter by chapter, has been its own kind of reverse-engineering—taking apart the experiences, examining the code of my own life, the bugs, the features, the unexpected crashes, and the surprising reboots.

If there's one thing this journey has taught me, it's that the "Hacker's Edge" isn't just about understanding technology or breaking systems. It's a way of seeing the world. It's about recognizing that you might have an edge in life that few others possess – a unique perspective, a relentless drive, an unconventional skill set forged in unorthodox crucibles like IRC channels instead of Ivy League halls. And it's about having the guts to lean into that edge, to trust it, and to use it to write your own goddamn rules and blaze your own path, even when the world tells you you're doing it wrong.

My path has been anything but linear. It's been a messy, often painful, sometimes hilarious, and frequently "impossibly random and beautifully fucked-up" ride, just as I recognized in that sushi bar in Bangalore. I've hit rock bottom more than once. I've failed spectacularly. I've been the outsider, the underdog, the one who didn't fit the mold. And if you're reading this and nodding along, if any part of that resonates deep in your bones, then this is for you.

To the next Ryans, the misfits, the rebels, the self-taught dreamers: your journey doesn't have to look like anyone else's. Your "GED" – whatever unconventional path or perceived disadvantage you carry – can become your badge of resilience, your unique strength. The system might not always recognize your worth at first glance. You might have to fight harder, be more persistent, and like me, go through hundreds of rejections before you find that one "yes." But that fierce independence, that refusal to quit when the odds are stacked against you? That's your superpower. Let your scoreboard, your results, do the talking.

Never stop looking for a better way to do things. That's the core of the hacker spirit. Question the status quo. Challenge assumptions. If a process is broken, fix it. If a system is inefficient, rebuild it. And if things are not working in your own life, in your career, in your relationships – don't be afraid to stop what you're doing, to pivot, and to take a different path. That's not failure; that's iteration. That's learning. That's growth.

My "why" for building and striving has evolved over the years. It started as a kid seeking control in a chaotic world, morphed through ambition and the thrill of the game, and has now settled into something more grounded: building a sustainable future for my family, finding a healthier balance between the relentless drive and the quiet joys of life. It's less about becoming a billion-dollar executive and more about crafting a life rich in purpose, connection, and presence.

The fight for your mind, body, and spirit isn't a detour; it's the most critical work you'll ever do. The most important startup you'll ever scale is yourself. Invest in that. Nurture it. Be as relentless in your pursuit of well-being as you are in your pursuit of success. Because ultimately, they are intertwined. So, what's the grand takeaway from my hacker's edge? It's this:

Embrace your unique perspective.

Don't let anyone else define your potential or your path. The detours, the mistakes, the moments you feel like you're breaking – those are often where the real learning happens, where your true strength is forged. Find your edge, whatever it may be, and lean into it with everything you've got.

The game of life will keep throwing you pitches. Some you'll crush. Some you'll whiff. Keep swinging anyway.

Build. Break. Learn. Repeat.

The edge is yours.

Take it.

ACKNOWLEDGEMENT

Thank you to Ellen Leanse for looking over the book and giving feedback.

Also thank you to Marcus Carey for writing the forward.

If you have helped me along my crazy path — THANK YOU.

ABOUT THE AUTHOR

Ryan Merket

Ryan has founded multiple startups, two of which were successfully sold, and he was fortunate enough to join Facebook's Platform team in its early days.

He later served as one of the first PMs and the leader of Ads Products at Reddit, one of the early members of the Amazon AWS Startup Team, and now helps high-potential startups for Microsoft for Startups. Ryan relocated to Austin after spending a decade in the San Francisco Bay Area to be closer to his family and to support startup founders in Texas.

Ryan is also a prolific angel investor and founder mentor, investing in hundreds of technology startups across the world.

In addition to his professional achievements, Ryan is an active father to his two children, Charlie and Stella, a life partner to Jenn Merket, and always has his dog, Wally, by his side.

He also has a bunch of side projects: JudeAI.com, CustomColoringPages.com, and ComalVentures.com

Extra page the publisher made me include. Feel free to rip this out and use it to pass notes in class or write a sweet note to your partner.